THE 17th/21st LANCERS

THE 17th/21st LANCERS

by
R.L.V. FFRENCH BLAKE

LEO COOPER
LONDON

First published in Great Britain 1968
by Hamish Hamilton Ltd
Republished in this revised edition 1993
by Leo Cooper
190 Shaftesbury Avenue, London, WC2H 8JL
an imprint of Pen & Sword Books Ltd.,
47 Church Street, Barnsley, S70 2AS

A CIP catalogue record of this book is available from the British Library

ISBN 0 85052 272 2

Typeset by Yorkshire Web, Barnsley, in 10 point Plantin

Printed by Redwood Books,
Trowbridge, Wiltshire.

CONTENTS

FOREWORD

by John Keegan

The regiment is a peculiarly British institution. Other armies have regiments, some of great antiquity, but none bear the distinguishing marks that make the British regiment into the brotherhood of warriors that it is. The chief distinguishing mark is stability, conferred by the practice of enlistment by the individual in one regiment for the whole of his service. A second is territorial association, by which a regiment draws its members from the same region. A third is autonomy, a degree of self-government in choosing its members and regulating its internal affairs, including even succession to command. A fourth is individuality in dress, customs, drill and forms of address, which emphasise the difference between one regiment and another.

There are other characteristics but these are the most important. They have been acquired gradually. Officers, until the abolition of purchase in 1871, exchanged between regiments quite frequently, while cavalry regiments associated themselves with recruiting areas only after the Second World War. From early times, however, regimental individuality was pronounced, so much so that the evolution of the regiment into its distinctive modern form may be said to have been a natural development. The British regiment is an organic, not a statutory organisation, which has grown into what it is, deriving its nature from a variety of origins and influences.

The history of the 17th/21st Lancers exemplifies the pattern of regimental development in all its complexity. Under its present title it dates from the amalgamations of historic cavalry regiments in 1922. The 17th Lancers had originally been Light Dragoons, raised for the Seven Years' War in 1759 and transformed into lancers after Waterloo. The 21st had had several incarnations, regiments of Light Dragoons with that number having been raised and disbanded during the Seven Years' War, the American War of Independence and the Napoleonic Wars. Most recently the 21st had begun as a regiment of the Honourable East India Company, the 3rd Bengal European Cavalry. It was brought on to the British establishment at the Company's dissolution, after the end of the Mutiny, and was entitled Light Dragoons and Hussars before becoming Lancers in 1897. As a former Indian regiment it brought with it traces of the French grey and silver uniform of the Company's cavalry, which derived in turn from that of Louis XV's hussars, introduced into the sub-continent by the French adventurers who were Clive's opponents in the struggle for control of the Moghul empire. That was not its only connection with the Moghul past. The title of Empress of India assumed by Queen Victoria, which she used in honouring the 21st for its distinction in the battle of Omdurman, was a revival of that borne by the Moghuls. Since the Moghuls claimed descent from Genghis Khan, the 21st preserve an association with the most ferocious light horsemen the world has ever known.

Being light horse, both the 17th and 21st have an extensive history of participation in imperial campaigns far from home, to which heavy cavalry was unsuited. America figures in their past to an unusual degree. The 17th saw out much of the American War of Independence. It also took part in the expedition to the River Plate of 1806-7, as did the 21st in its second incarnation, a strange episode from which Britain's troubled relationship with Argentina dates. The 17th campaigned widely in India, during the Company's wars of conquest and pacification in the early nineteenth century, and returned for the Mutiny, in which the 3rd Bengal European Cavalry was raised. Both regiments were to fight in Africa, against the Zulus, Sudanese and Boers; in the second Sudanese campaign the 21st mounted one of the most famous and one of the last decisive charges delivered by British cavalry.

The regiment which came into existence in 1922 had, therefore, a heritage of service perhaps more varied than that of any other in the cavalry of the line. It also had outstanding distinctions, notably from the Crimea where it had charged in the Light Brigade at Balaclava. Its imperial involvement had kept it outside Europe during the Napoleonic Wars, while the nature of the First World War had deprived it of the chance to operate in its traditional role on those battlefields. In the Second World War, however, it was to win new and great distinction, particularly in the bitter battles around the Kasserine Pass in Tunisia in 1943, and then in the long struggle for Italy on terrain so menacing to armoured units.

The regiment's last commitment before amalgamation was in Operation Granby in the Gulf War, where a detachment took part in what will come to be recognised as the most perfectly executed offensive in the history of armoured warfare. Now it is to amalgamate with the 16th/5th Lancers, with which it fought in Tunisia. It brings to the amalgamation not only its ancestral honours and its imperial traditions but also its distinctive regimental character. It is a strongly family regiment, in which many men with the same name have served over several generations. It has become firmly territorial, with its roots in the central shires. It has highly distinctive customs and unique peculiarities, notably the most widely recognised cap badge in the army. It is, above all, a happy regiment, not only a brotherhood of warriors but a genuine community of past and present members and of their kith and kin. The 17th/21st Lancers exemplifies the regimental system at its best. Its friends will wish it a splendid new future in its incarnation as the Queen's Royal Lancers.

Introduction

WITH THE impending amalgamation of the Regiment with the 16th/5th Royal Lancers, the title of 17th/21st Lancers will disappear for ever from the Army List. It has therefore been thought fitting to bring this short history up to date by adding one more chapter to cover the years since 1963. The book originally appeared as one of the "Famous Regiments" series published by Leo Cooper.

In writing this history of the Regiment, in which four generations of my family have had the honour to serve, I found myself faced with several problems. First, the need to condense some quarter-million words by previous historians, into the thirty thousand permitted by the publishers; secondly, the need to balance between chronicles of movements of troops and squadrons, and descriptions of the men who led them and fought in them; thirdly, my dislike of histories which describe operations in a campaign without enabling the reader to visualize how and where these actions fit into the campaign as a whole; lastly, my desire to include some account of the development of the cavalry as a whole during the period covered by the book. It is for this reason that I have included much detail about mechanization and early efforts at tank tactics.

In the 17th/21st we are lamentably short of documents – our regimental papers were repeatedly sunk at sea; we have no Rifleman

Harris; we are short of local colour; many of our campaigns were fought in remote corners of the globe, seldom in Europe; first-hand accounts are rare.

When it comes to dealing with personalities, I find myself at a loss. Out of 40 Colonels of the Regiment, over 100 Commanding Officers, 9 recipients of the VC, scores of other decorations and awards, whom to include, whom to omit? Anyone seeking these sort of details must turn to the Regimental Histories proper: there is space here only for the most famous. Here I am concerned with the Regiment as a whole — or rather Regiments, for we were two until amalgamation in 1922.

In the account of the Second World War, the reader will find divisions and brigades mentioned as frequently as squadrons and troops. The reason for this is that modern war has become increasingly a matter of intimate teamwork by all arms. Thus the history of the 17th/21st in the Second World War is inseparable from the history of the 6th Armoured Division. It is this very fact which is causing the slow eclipse of the regimental system — a system however which carries inherent qualities of tradition and continuity which in my opinion, are irreplaceable in the creation and maintenance of morale. Whoever is bold enough to abolish the system must take good care to put something effective in its place.

Loddon Lower Farm
Spencer's Wood
Reading, Berkshire
1993   R. L. V. ffrench Blake

Chapter One

The Birth of the Regiment

ON SEPTEMBER 13, 1759 General Wolfe lay dying on the Plains of Abraham beneath the walls of Quebec. His victory, which sealed the conquest of Canada, had been helped by the brilliant performance of the 47th Regiment of Foot, commanded by Colonel John Hale, This young man had served with the 47th as an Ensign during the Rebellion of '45, and had been ordered to America in 1752. Hale was a close personal friend of Wolfe's, and before the battle of Quebec, had tried to persuade him not to wear a new uniform, which might make him particularly conspicuous to the enemy. Wolfe's last despatches, written four days before the battle, had been expressed in a gloomy vein; he had been ill and dispirited; now he was dead, and it must have been with a heavy heart that Hale took ship for London, bearing these despatches, and the news of the victory. Perhaps as Canada sank below the horizon, Hale's thoughts turned to what the future might hold for him. For a Colonel to carry despatches was rather unusual; the bearer of tidings of victory could reasonably hope for some advancement or promotion. The ship docked on October 13; Hale delivered his despatches, and awaited his reward. Three weeks later he received it — a gratuity of £500, ten thousand acres of land in Canada, and a commission to raise one of five new regiments of Light Dragoons.

The British cavalry as we know it today dated from 1645, the year in which the Parliamentary Army fighting against Charles I was remodelled. Oliver Cromwell, then a captain, had raised and trained two cavalry regiments, so well disciplined, and so effective in battle, as to earn from Prince Rupert, the opposing cavalry leader, the nickname of Ironsides. These two regiments were combined into Sir Thomas Fairfax's Regiment of Horse, and became the first pattern of the modern cavalry unit.

The troopers wore scarlet coats, faced with their Colonel's colours. In the field they wore cuirasses and helmets of iron, and carried a brace of pistols and a long straight sword. Their horses were under fifteen hands high. The regiment contained six troops of one hundred men; one troop was commanded by the colonel, one by a major, and four by captains. In addition, there was one lieutenant and one quartermaster to each troop. The men formed up in five ranks of twenty, a horse's length apart and between files, leaving room for each horse to turn in its own length. Wheeling was difficult, but if it was attempted, the ranks were brought to close order, knee to knee, and nose to croup.

The troop was therefore the equivalent of a modern squadron, capable of being detached for long periods independently from the regiment. The firearm was the important weapon – the lance was totally obsolete and was never used. In action, the first rank fired their pistols, and filed round to the rear to reload. In the charge, the pistol was fired, thrown in the enemy's face, and the sword drawn. Training methods were somewhat primitive – as will be shown by the following cure for 'napping' or refusing to go forward:

'If your horse be resty so as he cannot be put forward then let one take a cat tied by the tail to a long pole, and when he goes backward, thrust the cat within his tail where she may claw him, and forget not to threaten your horse with a terrible noise. Or otherwise take on a hedgehog and tie him strait by one of his feet to the horse's tail, so that he may squeal and prick him.'

Each troop of cavalry, and company of infantry had its own standard – called in the cavalry a Cornet from its crescent shape, and in the infantry an Ensign. The junior lieutenant who carried it was in consequence known as the Cornet or Ensign – a term which survived for many years after the abolition of the standards

2

themselves. Half-way between the cavalry and the infantry lay the mounted infantry or dragoons. These were armed and drilled as infantry; they carried Ensigns, and were controlled by the drum and not by the cavalry trumpet. They fought on foot, using the horse only as a means of transport, dismounting to go into battle, and handing over ten horses to one horse-holder. The horses were poor animals, not up to cavalry standard and could not have shown much spirit, or this manoeuvre would hardly have been possible.

The two types of mounted unit, cavalry and dragoons, were both what would be termed 'heavy cavalry' – ponderous and inflexible in manoeuvre. In 1745, the Duke of Kingston, who had fought abroad and studied the cavalry tactics of foreign armies, being impressed by the light Hussars of other countries, raised at his own expense a regiment of Light Horse, and led it in the campaign against Scotland. Although this unit was disbanded two years later after fighting in Flanders, the seed of the light cavalry idea was sown; ten years later, each of the eleven cavalry regiments then extant, was augmented by the addition of a troop of Light Dragoons, sixty-five men strong. These Light Dragoons carried carbine and bayonet, pistols, axe, hedging-bill and spade. They were expected to fire from the saddle if necessary, and their mounts, instead of being heavy cart cobs, were of the 'nag or hunter kind' between 14.3 and 15.1 hands. All horses were docked short and had to be bought for a top price of twenty guineas.

The chief distinction of dress was that Light Dragoons wore helmets of strong leather – rather than the hats worn by the rest of the army.

Light cavalry carried a standard known as the 'guidon' (from the Italian 'guidone') – originally one to every troop, but after 1751 only three to a regiment, known as the King's, the Second and the Third.

So successful were the Light Dragoon troops in action that in 1759 King George II decided to raise two complete regiments – the 15th and 16th. Shortly after John Hale's arrival in England, the King reviewed the 15th and was so impressed with their training that he decided to raise five more Regiments. There was some

3

confusion at first, the title of 17th being allotted to two troops raised by Lord Aberdour, described by Fortescue as 'an apology for a corps'. However this 'corps' — mostly of disaffected Scotsmen — was eventually disbanded and in 1763 Hale's regiment, initially known as the 18th, now received its final precedence.

On the day of commissioning, the Board of General Officers met to decide upon the uniform for the new regiment:- scarlet coat, white facings, white lace with a black edge, in mourning for General Wolfe. Colonel Hale chose for a badge the Death's Head with the motto 'Or Glory', which has remained unchanged for over two hundred years, except that Hale's badge had the bones above the skull.

The Death's Head has been used as an emblem of victory by the warriors of primitive tribes for thousands of years; later it became the ensign of pirates and other desperadoes. It seems to have been first used as a military badge in 1741 by the 'Totenkopf' Hussars in Frederick the Great's Army. Deriving from the German word, the regimental nickname today is 'The Tots' and not the commonly heard 'Death or Glory Boys'. The Death's Head has since been used by Germans, Swedes, Spaniards, Poles, Frenchmen, Hitler's S.S. and by one other British regiment — the 24th Light Dragoons, raised in 1794 and disbanded in 1802. Colonel John Hale then received his warrant for arming the regiment — of 'four troops of 3 sergeants, 3 corporals, 2 drummers and 67 private men in each troop, besides commissioned officers' — to receive '300 pairs of pistols, 292 carbines, 292 cartouche boxes, and 8 drums'.

Hale next set out to raise the men in his home country of Hertfordshire. The Light Dragoon was required to be 'light and straight, and by no means gummy' — not under 5 feet 5½ nor over 5 feet 9 inches in height. Recruits were usually offered a bounty of three guineas, or more if the Colonel could afford it. The 17th was brought up to strength in seventeen days, and marched through Stratford to Coventry, where the establishment was increased to six troops, each troop also being raised in strength by half as much again. The 17th Light Dragoons — 21 officers, 678 rank and file, and one surgeon, had now come to life.

At almost the same time, that celebrated soldier, Lieutenant-General the Marquis of Granby, had been given permission to raise the fifth of the new regiments, the 21st Light Dragoons. It was to be commanded by his brother, Robert Manners-Sutton, who recruited his men from the family estates in Rutland and Lincolnshire, and his horses from 'among the finest hunters in the kingdom'. The regiment was given the title 'The Royal Foresters', with the motto 'Hic et Ubique'; the uniform bore dark blue facings. The 21st was raised in Nottingham and today the regimental museum has returned to the home of the founder — Belvoir Castle. In it can be seen three of the original guidons of the 21st Lancers.

There must have been much to do in those early days. The Colonel had to provide horses, saddlery, swords, and uniform, consisting of coat, waistcoat, breeches and cloak, knee-boots, boot-stockings, gloves, comb, forage cap, helmet and stable frock. The soldier received pay at the rate of 5d. a day 'subsistence', 2d. a day 'arrears', and about three farthings a day 'grass money' — a total annual wage of £13 14s. 10d. Out of this he had to buy what were called 'necessaries' — shirts, stockings, shoes, stock, breeches, buckles, gaiters and the inevitable cleaning materials, totalling £4 7s. 1d., and for his horse and his weapons, hoofpick, oil-bottle, grooming kit, saddle-bags, etc., adding up to a further fifteen shillings or so. Twopence a day was stopped for his food, and His Majesty took a shilling in the pound from the pay of every man in the army.

Training consisted of weapon drill, some sort of riding instruction under a riding master, and plenty of musketry (including firing from the saddle), for which Light Dragoons received an extra allotment of ammunition. In the 'grass season' from May till October, the horses were turned out with a 'grass guard', and training was confined to dismounted exercises. Barrack life and stable routine must have been similar to, though more primitive than, the way of life in the cavalry which continued for nearly two hundred years, until the beginning of the Second World War. Since then only the Household Cavalry have continued to be equipped with horses. Standing Orders of 1760 lay down the hours as: Reveille 5.30, morning stables 8 a.m., evening stables 4 p.m., 'rack up' 8 p.m., 'tattoo' (or 'tap-to' meaning no more liquor to be drawn), 9 p.m. In the barrack rooms, crammed with arms, equipment and saddlery, men slept two or more in a bed, and the struggle to keep equipment and clothing clean and tidy must have been even harder than it is today. But standards in the Light Dragoons were high. Each man's furlough paper bore a note requesting any officer who read it, to report if the bearer were 'unsoldierly in dress or manner'. Hair was to be worn long, under the hat, and on parade it was plaited in a 'queue', hanging at full length or doubled into a 'club'. Powder on the hair was permitted, but no grease. Cutting the hair was strictly forbidden, except in cases of sickness, when a wig was provided. Punishment was by fine, or by confinement in a Black Hole, 'free from damp, as dark and dismal as possible where clean dry straw is to be put every week'. Normal punishments were 24 hours in the Black Hole for a first offence, 48 hours for the second, and trial by Court Martial for the third. A shilling fine was the penalty for swearing – 'a custom', according to Regimental Standing Orders of 1768, 'which is wicked, unsoldierlike, and directly contrary to the Articles of War'. Trial by Court Martial might lead to punishment by flogging, the sentence being executed on parade, with the victim strung up in the centre of a hollow square.

Marriage was discouraged, and the number of married men was controlled strictly for many years. Once officially married, a soldier might have his wife to live in the barrack room, and was allowed to screen off his bed from the rest of the room. The wife was expected to wash, cook and mend, and to help keep clean her husband's one suit of uniform. Standing orders forbade the carrying of coals or other dirty loads – including children! – while in regimental clothes. Entertainment must have been scarce (other than women and drink), for those same Standing Orders lay down that 'all men are to return to their quarters whenever there is any mob, bull-baiting, or football match, on pain of being confined for disobedience of orders'.

The Light Dragoon regiments had been raised for service in the

Seven Years War, but neither the 17th nor the 21st was sent abroad, though both furnished drafts of men and horses. In 1763 the war came to an end, and many regiments were disbanded, among them the 21st Light Dragoons. When the order was received at Nottingham, they 'refused to be broke', and three troops of the 3rd Hussars had to be sent to 'assist in forcing them'. The 17th, however, survived. John Hale was promoted to full Colonel, and married Mary Chaloner of Guisborough. From now on, the founder gradually fades from regimental history. He had left the regiment in 1762 to serve as Military Secretary to Lord Albemarle in Havannah, where he appears to have acquired a considerable fortune. On his return he turned his attention to family life; Mrs Hale bore him twenty-one children, most of whom survived. His grant of land in Canada lapsed to the Crown, but several of his sons acquired property in that country. No son of his served with the regiment, possibly due to the fact that his successor as Colonel was George Preston of the Scots Greys. Hale had a bitter hatred of the Scots, founded on his memories of the '45 Rebellion. Also, while the regiment was serving in Scotland in 1761, Hale and four brother officers had ridden down a toll-keeper who tried to stop them on the way back to their quarters. This escapade cost them a fine of £230, and a public reprimand from the King. Hale was later appointed to a Governorship in Ireland, and was promoted to full General, eventually dying at the age of 78, 'leaving behind him seventeen children, and the 17th Light Dragoons'.

The period after the Seven Years War was spent in reforms and reorganization within the cavalry, including technical improvements in saddlery; the introduction of trumpeters to the Light Dragoons – one to each troop, who when dismounted formed a 'band of music', the forerunners of the regimental bands; and most important, the introduction of more flexible drill in the field.

Now in 1773, rumours of trouble in the American colonies began to reach England. In 1774 seven infantry regiments were despatched to America, and a year later, the 17th, at that time in Ireland, 'a very fine regiment, and fit for service' (according to its inspection report), was brought up to strength with drafts and ordered to embark at Cork for the port of Boston.

Chapter Two

The American War

THE 17TH TRAVELLED to America in seven little ships — embarking six troops, each of two officers, five NCOs, twenty-six dragoons and thirty-one horses. An officer had already gone on ahead to Boston to make arrangements and to buy horses — Oliver De Lancey, an American, born in New York, educated in England, and now a captain in the 17th. Two months later, when the little convoy sailed into Boston, he must have been on the quay with the news that war had broken out — he could buy no horses — in any case no horses were needed, for Boston was under siege. Two days later, the 17th, busy disembarking, finding billets, stables and forage, must have left their work to watch 2,500 of General Gage's infantry, supported by artillery and warships, crossing the quarter-mile strait to Charlestown, and struggling up the slopes of the two hills which overlooked Boston — Breed's and Bunker. If the Generals — Gage, Howe and Clinton — expected a walk-over, they were to receive a shock. The untrained Americans held their fire like veterans, and the British lost a thousand men before they took Bunker Hill. The Americans, described by Wolfe as 'the worst soldiers in the universe', were to show that patriots, fighting in their own country, can in the end defeat the best troops. The British won many more battles, but in the end, they lost the war.

On the map overleaf is a rough outline of those campaigns of the

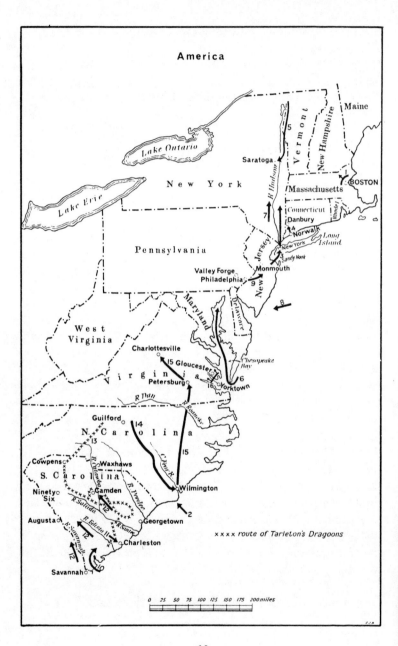

America

Maine

Lake Ontario

New York

Vermont

New Hampshire

Saratoga

BOSTON

Massachusetts

Lake Erie

Connecticut

Danbury

Norwalk

Rhode

Pennsylvania

Long Island

New York

Sandy Hook

Valley Forge
Philadelphia

Monmouth

Maryland

West
Virginia

Delaware

Chesapeake Bay

Charlottesville

Gloucester

Virginia

Petersburg

Yorktown

R Dan

R Roanoke

Guilford

N. Carolina

Cowpens

Waxhaws

S. Carolina

R Catawba

R Pee Dee

Wilmington

Ninety
Six

Camden

R Santee

R Saluda

Augusta

R Edisto

Georgetown

R Savannah

Charleston

Savannah

×××× route of Tarleton's Dragoons

0   25   50   75   100   125   150   175   200 miles

10

American Revolution, with which we are concerned in this book. The sequence of events was as follows (*numbers refer to map*):

1. April 1775. Continued unrest, caused by heavy taxation to pay for Imperial defence, now breaks out into open rebellion. Citizens arming everywhere. Expedition to safeguard large magazine at Concord, twenty miles from Boston, meets militia at Lexington. Firing begins, British are harassed all the way back to Boston, and besieged. General Gage is British C.-in-C.

March 1776, Boston evacuated, army removed to Halifax, Nova Scotia.

2. December 1775. Governor of North Carolina asks for help to rally Tory loyalists. Five infantry regiments under Lord Cornwallis sent from England to Cape Fear. General Clinton takes command. Attempt to capture Charleston fails disastrously after unsuccessful naval action against forts. Loyalist support proves disappointing.

3 & 4. August 1776. General Howe, now C-in-C, sends force to capture Long Island and New York, and later operates north and west of New York, and in Connecticut. 17th in action for the first time.

5. June 1777. General Burgoyne advances southwards down the Hudson, expecting Howe to drive northwards to meet him.

6. July 1777. Howe, instead of supporting Burgoyne, sails to the Chesapeake and captures Philadelphia. Burgoyne, struggling in impossible country, surrenders at Saratoga in October 1777.

7. October 1777. Clinton's expedition to the Hudson highlands, in support of Burgoyne, is too little and too late. British remain inactive all winter at Philadelphia. American army in poor condition only twenty-five miles away at Valley Forge.

8. February 1778. France sides with the rebels, French fleet sent to American coast, depriving Britain of absolute command of the sea. War now 'escalating' to all western world.

9. May 1778. Clinton succeeds Howe as British C-in-C, and is forced to send troops to Europe and West Indies to meet French threats. Evacuates Philadelphia and fights way out, through Monmouth, to Sandy Hook and New York. To compensate for

11

loss of regular troops, mixed corps or 'legions' of loyal American light infantry and dragoons, with stiffening of British cavalry, formed in New York, and trained in summer 1770. 17th attached to 'British Legion' commanded by Banastre Tarleton.

10. February 1779. Clinton's army lands at Savannah for a second attempt at a campaign in Carolinas.

11. May 1779. Charleston captured.

12. May 1779. Clinton sends columns inland to Augusta, Ninety-Six and Camden, latter commanded by General Cornwallis.

13. May 1779-January 1881. Route taken by Tarleton's Legion fighting in support of Cornwallis.

14. February 1781. Cornwallis' army, exhausted, withdraws to Wilmington.

15. May 1781. Virginia Campaign. Cornwallis marches from Wilmington to Petersburg and Charlottesville.

16. September 1781. Yorktown Campaign. Cornwallis withdraws to Yorktown, is besieged and surrenders. Tarleton's Legion surrenders at Gloucester.

The 17th remained besieged in Boston, where they spent eight wretched months without fresh food for themselves, with little forage for their horses. Eventually they were evacuated with the rest of the army to Halifax, in Nova Scotia. Here the 16th Light Dragoons arrived from England with a consignment of remounts; but 412 horses out of 950 had died on the voyage, so the 17th were still poorly mounted. An increase in strength of thirty men per troop was authorized, but these reinforcements had not been received by the time the regiment sailed for the capture of New York.

Howe's army landed at Sandy Hook and was transferred to Staten Island, from where the attack on Long Island was launched. The crossing in boats and barges started at dawn, the 17th landing on the first day. The enemy force occupied a line of hills called the Heights of Guian, behind which lay Brooklyn. Howe's plan was to feint at the American right, which rested on the river, and then to outflank their left with a 'right hook' directed on Jamaica Pass, some five miles to the east. De Lancey, the New Yorker, led the advanced guard of the 17th which brushed aside an American patrol and found the pass unoccupied. Howe, rolling up the enemy line from the east, had 12,000 of the Americans pinned in the Brooklyn with their backs to the East River; and then he let them escape tamely by boat to Manhattan Island, with the loss of three stragglers and five cannon too heavy to manhandle across the mud!

With Long Island gone, the Americans evacuated Manhattan Island and withdrew to the north. The 17th took part in several minor operations under Cornwallis during the pursuit, providing the General with a detachment for special duties, probably escort and communications. A member of this party, Private M'Mullins, carrying a special letter to an outpost, was ambushed and fired on. He at once resorted to a trick he had learned in the riding school, of hanging head down from the saddle. When the enemy ran out to get him, he sat up again, shot one with his carbine, one with his pistol, and drew his sword on the other two, who surrendered. M'Mullins was promoted to sergeant by the Commander-in-Chief, and commended to the King. Detachments of the 17th took part in two other affairs in the New York campaign – the first a raid on an enemy magazine at Danbury by a force landed on the shores of Long Island sound at Norwalk, and the second, the storming of Fort Clinton in the expedition to the Hudson Highlands. At the end of this phase of the war, the 17th moved to Philadelphia during the winter of 1777, and when spring came, took part in offensive operations designed to keep open communications around the city. Among these engagements was the attack at Crooked Billet on May 1, when an American post of 450 militia was routed, and all their baggage captured with the loss of only nine British casualties.

On May 18, some officers of the Regiment took part in a fantastic pageant organized by Captains John André and Oliver De Lancey – the entertainment which was known as the *Mischianza* (Italian for 'mix-up'). André, a British infantry captain, of Swiss birth, later, as Clinton's Adjutant-General, became involved in the strange affair of the treason of the American general, Benedict Arnold.

While acting as emissary, he was arrested as a spy and executed by the Americans in 1780.

Now in May of 1778, he directed this grand regatta, and mock tournament between the 'Knights of the Blended Roses and the Burning Mountains' led by Lord Cathcart of the 17th. The costumes of the knights and their ladies, and of the soldiers dressed as squires and pages, are said to have cost £12,000. The expenses were borne by twenty-two field officers! While this extravaganza (created to mark the departure of General Howe as Commander-in-Chief in America), was still in full swing, Washington sent the newly arrived French General Lafayette with 2,000 men to Barren Hill, eleven miles from Philadelphia, on a 'reconnaissance in force' to report on the prospects of the British leaving the city. On the outskirts of Philadelphia Allen McLane, the American partisan leader, simulated an attack by galloping along the British outpost line dropping gunpowder bombs and scrap metal, and causing some alarm at the *Mischianza*. Next evening, the British set out with a force of 5,000 men to surround Lafayette; but McLane's outposts gave warning and the Americans slipped away, only the rear-guard being caught by the 17th, who took forty prisoners.

A month later, the evacuation of Philadelphia was begun; the British started on an arduous march across country to Sandy Hook, some seventy miles away. These operations are known as the Monmouth Campaign. The 17th had the duty of protecting the twelve mile long baggage column (which was sent on ahead), while the 16th were employed on flank- and rear-guard tasks. After ten days' marching, the two armies met and Clinton turned at Monmouth to offer battle to the Americans. Recalling the 17th from their duties with the baggage column nine miles ahead, he ordered them into the rear guard, and used both of his light dragoon regiments as a screen against the American cavalry. The Americans refused to accept battle with Clinton's strong defensive positions at Monmouth, so he attacked them three times with his infantry, driving them back in intense heat to the heights of Freehold. It was a classic rearguard disengagement action, for the Americans dropped the pursuit, and the British reached Sandy Hook and the safety of their barges without further interference. The 17th had no casualties at Freehold. The regiment went into winter quarters on Long Island, taking over all the horses and some men of the 16th, who now had gone home to England. The summer of 1779 was spent in outpost and foraging work in the country north of New York. The most notable event for the 17th was the capture of a small American fort by Sergeant Thomas Tucker and twelve men; for which feat he was awarded a commission as Cornet in the regiment.

The British now turned their efforts to the Carolinas, and Clinton prepared again to capture Charleston. It was not however until Boxing Day 1779 that his army, including a troop of sixty 17th Light Dragoons, sailed from New York, only to be caught in a severe storm. All the cavalry horses died, and a ship containing siege artillery was lost. The troop of 17th was attached to Banastre Tarleton's 'British Legion', which landed at Savannah, a hundred miles to the south of Charleston.

Banastre Tarleton, 26 years old, was the son of a rich Liverpool merchant. Originally commissioned in the King's Dragoon Guards, he volunteered for service in America, sailed with Clinton's first expedition to Charleston, and was later posted to the 16th, where he soon proved himself efficient and dashing. Now he was Lieutenant-Colonel in charge of 'The British Legion', originally formed by Lord Cathcart of the 17th. The Legion wore a distinctive green uniform, and contained both light infantry and dragoons. The 17th were attached, and wore their own uniform — moreover when it wore out they refused to wear the green of the Legion, but insisted on patching up their own scarlet.

Tarleton's Legion now started on a brilliant campaign, lasting until the surrender of Yorktown and covering at least fifteen hundred miles. The Legion first headed for Port Royal in requisitioned boats, scouring the islands to collect horses. They scraped together enough poor screws to remount the Green Dragoons and the 17th. Tarleton joined General James Paterson's main force moving on Charleston; an attack by irregular horsemen was repulsed by the 17th, who gained the valuable prize of more horses. Clinton now turned against the landward defences of Charleston, which consisted of fortifications, guarded by a screen of three regiments of cavalry, commanded by General Huger. Tarleton's Legion was despatched against this force, the infantry and cavalry of which were divided by the River Cooper. On April 12 Tarleton headed for the bridge at Monck's Corner, and with typical dash, pushed on through the night and fell on the main guard of the enemy cavalry in the dark at 3 a.m. The surprise attack was a complete success; the Legion smashed their way into the enemy's camp, taking 150 prisoners, 400 first-class horses, and 150 wagons of ammunition. Tarleton's dragoons crossed the bridge, seized Bowman's Ferry on another branch of the Cooper, and thus gained command of all landward communications to Charleston. Huger, and his second-in-command, Colonel William Washington (second cousin of George Washington), escaped by hiding in a swamp.

On May 11 the Charleston garrison capitulated, and Clinton despatched three columns inland, one up the Savannah River to Augusta (a Tory stronghold), one up the Saluda to Ninety-Six, and one (under Cornwallis) up the Santee towards Camden, in pursuit of Colonel Buford's Virginians, escorting the Governor of Charleston. Tarleton was ordered to join this last column; in his eagerness to catch a rebel governor, he not only forced the pace, but started with many of his horses carrying both a dragoon and an infantryman. Covering a hundred and five miles in fifty-four hours, leaving behind the infantrymen and his only three-pounder gun, he came on Buford's force at the little settlement of Waxhaws on May 29. Tarleton sent an officer forward with a flag of truce, as a stratagem to intimidate Buford into submission; but Buford continued his march and returned a defiance. Tarleton then deployed in three columns, with the 17th in the centre, and charged. The Americans held their fire too long, and were broken up completely. Tarleton's horse was killed under him, and his men, believing him dead, gave no quarter. The subsequent massacre became known as 'Tarleton's Quarter', and the commander of the Legion as 'Bloody Tarleton' for ever after.

From Waxhaws, they turned back to Camden on August 16; here Cornwallis defeated General Gates; the Legion was employed in the pursuit after the battle; the Americans lost two thousand men, and the British three hundred and fifty. Moving on from Camden, Tarleton was at once sent to find General Sumter – the 'Gamecock'. Giving chase with 350 men and one cannon, Tarleton saw enemy camp fires across the river at dusk. Bivouacking without fires or lights, he waited till dawn hoping that Sumter would ford the Wateree and expose his force to attack during the crossing. But the Americans continued up the west bank, so Tarleton crossed over and followed undetected to Fishing Creek. Here his exhausted foot soldiers gave up, and refused to go further. Tarleton put sixty of them to ride double behind his hundred dragoons, and rode on in the heat. Five miles on, the advance guard cut down two enemy scouts, and breasting a rise, found Sumter's force below on the river bank, sleeping, cooking and bathing, with arms stacked. Tarleton deployed at once and charged; Sumter, in his shirtsleeves, jumped bareback on to the nearest horse. The Legion, with a loss of sixteen killed and wounded, killed 150, captured 300, released 100 British prisoners, and captured 44 wagons of supplies.

This victory marked the peak of the Legion's achievement. Things never again went so easily for them; and the American forces gradually improved as they gained in skill and experience. Tarleton became desperately ill with a fever; the Legion, under his subordinates, performed rather badly in the King's Mountain campaign. Tarleton, partly recovered, then went south to chase, unsuccessfully, Francis Marion, the 'Swamp Fox', in the hinterland behind Georgetown. The Legion was abruptly recalled from the marshes of the Lower Peedee, in order to find and disperse a force of a thousand rebels under Sumter. After the usual pattern of chase, Sumter turned to face Tarleton at Blackstocks on the Tyger River; the fighting was fierce, the marksmanship of the American riflemen stopped the British infantry, and Tarleton was forced to lead a desperate cavalry charge to extricate his infantry. Sumter was badly wounded, and in the darkness both sides withdrew.

In December, Clinton, now at Winnsboro, was threatened by a

new enemy commander, Nathaniel Greene, a brilliant, and what is more, a thoughtful general. Greene's senior commander was Daniel Morgan (the 'Old Wagoner'), an experienced and cunning veteran. Greene, dividing his forces into two, sent Morgan across the River Catawba to operate in the Broad River basin, while he himself remained at Cheraw, on the Peedee River. Cornwallis, uncertain of Greene's intentions, sent Tarleton to destroy Morgan's force, which consisted of 600 Continentals (i.e. Regulars) and 300 militia. Morgan knew Tarleton would make an immediate frontal attack, and he therefore disposed his force cleverly among the trees on a little wooded hill known as the Cowpens. His regulars manned the crest, while the militia (of somewhat uncertain morale) were posted *in front* with orders to fire two volleys, picking out the officers and sergeants, and then to withdraw. Morgan gauged his men's morale well — he put them where they were forced to fight, with no swamp in sight to which they could run from the threat of the Legion's dragoons! Tarleton fell into the trap, his infantry were repulsed; his dragoons were struck in the flank by Morgan's cavalry; his reserve of infantry failed to push the attack home, and were charged in turn by Morgan's regulars.

The British line broke and ran, and the American cavalry, with Colonel William Washington at their head, came charging among them. Tarleton galloped over to fetch his own Green Dragoons, but all two hundred of them rode off and left him. Only the forty men of the 17th rallied round him, as he tried, too late, to save the guns. As Tarleton now started to retreat, Colonel Washington appeared in pursuit. For a moment the two leaders and their escorts were slashing furiously at each other; Tarleton fired a pistol at Washington, but missed; then he turned and galloped from the field. The rout of the Legion was complete; the irregular cavalry escaped, but the two infantry regiments, the 7th and 71st Foot, were cut to pieces, and never forgave Tarleton for abandoning them.

Cornwallis, thirty miles away, learned that the Legion was beaten, and started ponderously in pursuit of Morgan. But the 'Old Wagoner' was already heading north-east back to Virginia and the safety of the River Dan. Cornwallis picked up the trail, and forced the passage of the River Catawba, but at the River Yadkin he was blocked by high water, and shortage of boats. Tarleton's Legion was sent thirty miles upstream to a ford, but Morgan, fighting skilful rearguard actions, escaped across the Dan. As Cornwallis fell back from the pursuit, Nathaniel Greene followed him to Guilford on the Haw River. After a ferocious infantry battle, Greene was defeated, but the British forces were now so tired and weakened, that they could do no more. Cornwallis retired slowly down the river to Wilmington.

Greene returned to fight against Lord Rawdon in South Carolina; Cornwallis started on his ill-fated march to Virginia, a journey which ended in his surrender at Yorktown; Tarleton's Legion was also besieged, and forced to capitulate at Gloucester on the opposite side of the York River; the names of twenty-five of the 17th appearing on the roll of those who surrendered. Hostilities ended officially in April 1782. Captain Stapleton, of the 17th, handed the announcement to George Washington.

Tarleton was released on parole to England in 1782 and was appointed Colonel of the 21st Light Dragoons in 1802. He saw little active service again; his leadership of the Legion must rank him as one of the greatest of cavalry officers at regimental level. The 17th, at war for the first time, had served him well, and had proved themselves tough, reliable and efficient. Although dispersed in separate detachments over the whole American theatre, they clearly retained their strong regimental spirit. Decorations and citations for individual bravery were rare; we know only of M'Mullins, Tucker, and Corporal O'Lavery, who thrust an important message into a wound, to conceal it from the enemy, and died pointing out its 'ghastly hiding place'. But it is clear that in their first period of active service, the 17th had played their part splendidly.

Chapter Three

The West Indies

THE ENTRY OF THE FRENCH into the American War immediately raised the alarm of invasion in England. Three new regiments of light dragoons were at once formed; one, again numbered the 21st, was raised by Major-General John Douglas, with Philip de la Motte as Lieutenant-Colonel, and John Floyd as Major. The latter had been a cornet in the 15th Light Dragoons, and had ridden in the charge of Emsdorff at the age of *twelve*! An extract from his letters gives a hint of his keenness as a trainer of men: 'The 21st is new, the most willing people I ever saw and perfectly well behaved. They ride ill, but do their business in the field very well for all that, and are surprising well on foot. We staid out till 20th of November, and had hutted our tents, expecting to stay longer (December 1779)...I am at work with them every day, and they live on horseback, but having all the instructors to teach it is impossible to enter all into the detail I should wish. (January 1700)...the winter has been severe for England, however our ground was so favourable that I was constantly able to see the men on horseback five times a week...and I am well pleased with the appearance of them for the time' (March 1780). But in 1783 at the end of the war, the 21st was again disbanded.

The 17th arrived back in Ireland late in 1783, was reduced to peace establishment, and issued with the new light dragoon

John Hale, the founder of the 17th, by Sir Joshua Reynolds.
Reproduced by kind permission of the owner, A.R. Gillespie Esq., of Montreal.

A private soldier of the 17th Light Dragoons, 1759.
Reproduced by gracious permission of Her Majesty the Queen, from the original painting by David Morier.

John Manners, Marquis of Granby, the founder of the 21st Light Dragoons.
Engraved by Robinson from a portrait by Sir Joshua Reynolds.

A private soldier of the 21st (Granby's) Light Dragoons, 1760.
Reproduced by gracious permission of Her Majesty the Queen, from the original painting by David Morier.

Two splendid drawings from the sketchbooks of Captain
Thomas Ellis of the 17th Light Dragoons, showing the
change, between 1804 and 1806, from the handsome and
practical Light Dragoon helmet, to the tall ugly felt shako.
*Reproduced by the kind permission of the Directors of the
Parker Gallery.*

uniform of dark blue. Twelve years were spent with little incident, except 'aid to the civil power' in Belfast.

In 1793, war with France broke out again, and Britain set about capturing the French possessions in the West Indies. The campaign in San Domingo did not go well, so in 1795 it was decided to send four regiments of light dragoons, dismounted, to that island. A force of eight troops from the 13th, 17th and 18th was sent ahead, and after a terrible voyage arrived in Jamaica. Told that there had been an 'unfortunate blunder' they were sent off towards San Domingo, but some − including one troop of the 17th − were immediately recalled. The Maroons had rebelled, and the soldiers were needed immediately.

Meanwhile the rest of the regiment (four troops) sailed from Ireland to England, and joined the cavalry camp at Netley under Lord Cathcart. From there they sailed for the West Indies, the fleet again being dispersed by storm. Two troops were landed in Martinique, and two later in Grenada − probably the same two troops. The remainder of the regiment arrived in San Domingo. The 21st, raised for the third time by Colonel Beaumont in Yorkshire, was also in this convoy to San Domingo, and so for the first time the two regiments met each other.

The Maroons were the descendants of slaves who had escaped from the Spanish after the British conquest of Jamaica in 1658. About 1730, the various independent bands of these renegades had become united under a ruler of some genius called Cudjoe, who had taught them a particular type of warfare. Fortescue describes it thus:

> The grand object was to take up a central position in a 'cockpit' − i.e. a glen enclosed by perpendicular rocks, and accessible only through a narrow defile. A chain of such cockpits runs through the mountains from east to west, communicating by more or less practicable passes one with another...the sides are so steep as to be impassable to any but a Maroon...The outlets of these cockpits were so few that the white men could always find a well-beaten track which led

21

them to the mouth of a defile, but beyond the mouth they could not go. Warned by the horns of the scouts...the Maroons hid themselves in ambush behind rocks and trees, selected each his man, shot him down, and then vanished to some fresh position. Turn whither he might, the unlucky pursuer was met always by a fresh volley from an invisible foe, who never fired in vain.

These formidable jungle fighters had concluded a treaty with the King, and had been granted rights of self-government in 1738. But in the course of years, their internal discipline began to fall to pieces, and they began to become aggressive and dissatisfied. The Governor, Lord Balcarres, was aware that French agents were at work spreading sedition among the plantation natives, and he felt that a firm hand was necessary. He therefore blockaded the Maroon strongholds, and attacked the two Maroon towns. After a month, the British had lost two officers and seventy men killed in action, and many more from wounds and sickness, without one single proven Maroon casualty!

Operations at this point were handed over to a Colonel Walpole of the 13th Light Dragoons, who selected the troop of the 17th for special training as 'mountaineer marksmen' climbing, shooting, and adopting the enemy's ambush tactics. A young lieutenant, Oswald Werge, showed particular skill and bravery in an action when the Maroons, driven out of their cockpit by a howitzer manhandled up through the passes, occupied a 'stupendous height'. Werge discovered the path up it by observing a water-carrier, and the 17th drove the enemy off the heights; tactics which white men had never before attempted against the rebels. The Maroons eventually surrendered to Walpole, and begged for pardon. Walpole promised that they should not be sent out of the island; but the Jamaica Government failed to honour this agreement. Walpole therefore refused to accept a presentation sword, and resigned his commission in disgust.

In Grenada, the 17th took a leading part in the relief of the island from rebellious natives. In San Domingo five troops of the regiment fought the French — but a worse enemy, the yellow fever, inflicted far more casualties. A muster roll of December 1796 shows that in seven months, out of 12 sergeants, 7 died; 116 privates, 76 died; 2 trumpeters, both died.

At this point we must refer to a story originating in Cannon's Historical Record of the 17th Light Dragoons, where it is said that two troops of the 17th were employed for a time as Marines on board the *Hermione* frigate commanded by Captain Pigot, who was afterwards murdered by his own crew. Fortescue repeats this statement, which throws some light on an old regimental nickname — 'The Horse Marines'. In fact, Admiralty records show that the 17th never shipped in *Hermione*, but in another ship of Pigot's, H.M.S. *Success*; and that the regiment travelled as 'supernumeraries' not as replacements for marines. However, to this day the officers of the regiment keep the naval custom of remaining seated in the mess when the National Anthem is played; whether this practice dates from the 'Horse Marine' period is not known, but it is certain that the regiment spent a great deal of time at sea.

The 17th left the West Indies in 1797; on the voyage home, the headquarter ship, *Caledonia*, foundered. The men were saved, but all the baggage and regimental books were lost.

Chapter Four

South America

ON LANDING IN ENGLAND, the regiment, reduced to skeleton strength, was quartered at Nottingham, Leicester, Bath, Bristol, and Trowbridge; the officers set about bringing their men up to date with the new manual of sword-drill. The following year, 1798, one sergeant and eight men of the 17th took part in Sir Eyre Coote's abortive expedition, to capture Ostend, and to destroy the lock-gates at the entrance to the Bruges Canal. This scheme, the invention of Captain Sir Home Popham, R.N., was designed to prevent the French from using the canal as an invasion base. The expedition failed, and the entire force was taken prisoner. The men of the 17th seem to have conducted themselves well; Sergeant William Brown was commissioned, and all the others promoted to non-commissioned rank, after they had been exchanged and returned to England. The war ended, temporarily, at the Peace of Amiens in 1802, but fourteen months later, broke out again; the 17th, moving again to Ireland, prepared for service against Napoleon. But in spite of various false alarms, it was not until October of 1806 that the 17th embarked again for foreign service, without their horses, and with the surprising destination of South America.

In January 1806, a British force of 4,000 troops under Sir David Baird, convoyed by the same Sir Home Popham, had captured the Cape of Good Hope from the Dutch. The 21st formed part of this force. Sir Home Popham had, two years earlier, pressed the British Government to send an expedition to South America, where, he was convinced, the revolutionary elements would be encouraged to rise against Spain, the ruling power in that country. This plan had not met with approval; but now Popham, with really astounding boldness, persuaded Baird to let him have a force of nine hundred men, including two troops of the 21st, all under the command of Brigadier-General Beresford. He then sailed with this force and his own squadron, to capture Buenos Aires on his own responsibility! The plan succeeded, and in June of 1806, Beresford captured Buenos Aires.

As usual, the promised revolutionary support turned out to be a myth; in August the inhabitants of Buenos Aires, who had sworn allegiance to the King, rose and overwhelmed Beresford's force, which surrendered on condition that the army should be shipped off to England. The Spaniards, however, broke the agreement, and imprisoned the whole force and its commander, up country at Catamarca.

Popham's despatch, announcing his first victory, brought back the peremptory reply that he was to present himself in England for trial by court-martial. At the same time, however, a force under General Sir Samuel Auchmuty was ordered to sail as reinforcements for Beresford. After several changes of plan, this force, of some three thousand men, including the 17th Light Dragoons, sailed in October, still unaware of the disaster which had occurred in Buenos Aires.

Putting in at Rio de Janeiro for water, they learnt of Beresford's capture, and of the arrival of a small reinforcement of two regiments of infantry at Maldonado, at the mouth of the River Plate. Auchmuty sailed at once for Maldonado, where he arrived in January 1807. He picked up the two infantry regiments from this useless position, and sailed to attack Monte Video. He landed nine miles from the town, at Caretas Rocks, and three days later, deployed his force in two columns for the advance. The right column consisted of the 17th and two troops each of the 20th and 21st, all dismounted, the 17th armed curiously with Spanish muskets from Rio de Janeiro. An attack by four thousand Spanish cavalry was beaten off, and the column reached the suburbs of Monte Video that evening. Next morning, the enemy put in a holding attack against the dismounted cavalrymen, and made their main effort against the British infantry in the left column. The attack, by six thousand men, was defeated, with an enemy loss estimated at fifteen hundred. However, further probing into Monte Video revealed that the defences were not weak (as the optimistic Popham had suggested), but in Auchmuty's words, 'respectable' meaning 160 guns. Auchmuty laid siege to the defences, and after ten days' preparation sent his infantry into the assault; the cavalry, marines and one regiment of foot were used to protect the rear of the assault force, which stormed over the defences and quickly had command of the town.

A proportion of Auchmuty's cavalry soon mounted themselves on the local ponies. These were not really strong enough to carry a British dragoon with full equipment, and the cavalry must have looked comical enough on parade; while in the field they were troubled by the local irregulars – active horsemen and good shots, who were skilful at fighting skirmishing actions without getting caught. The two hundred mounted men of the 17th were sent up country to Canelones and San José, where forage was easier to find; while the dismounted cavalry remained in Monte Video.

The British Government was now dreaming of the conquest of all Spanish South America. General Craufurd, with four thousand men, was ordered to the Pacific to take Lima and Valparaiso – and to join up with Beresford across the continent – a mere thousand miles of mountain, forest and pampas! However, Craufurd's force was spared from rounding the Horn, for on arriving at the Cape of Good Hope, he found orders to join Auchmuty on the River Plate, where he eventually arrived in June 1807. Auchmuty meanwhile, having received further reinforcements, including the 9th Light Dragoons, had prepared for the capture of Buenos Aires by seizing Colonia, immediately opposite on the north bank of the river.

The British Government now sealed the fate of its forces in South

America, by the appointment over Auchmuty and Craufurd of the incompetent General John Whitelocke.

The army embarked at Colonia and Monte Video, and landed at Ensenada, on the south bank of the river, thirty miles east of Buenos Aires. The landing was met by Spanish light cavalry; here was the chance for the Light Dragoons, but General Whitelocke, with mounted men from four splendid regiments under his command, chose to employ them on other duties — to furnish pack-horses for the commissariat, to guard the landing of provisions, to carry despatches, to accompany the infantry brigades in 'penny packets' and to act as the General's personal bodyguard! The army stumbled across ditches and swamps, unprotected by its own cavalry and tormented by that of the enemy, while the dismounted light dragoons followed ignominiously as rearguard to the force. On July 3 General Whitelocke lost his army altogether; on July 4 he found it again; on July 5 he attacked the city; according to Fortescue 'he sent 6,000 men up fourteen different streets through three miles of a hostile town, with strict orders not to fire until they reached the far end'. By that time, a thousand had fallen; fifteen hundred more — including Craufurd himself — had been surrounded and forced to surrender. Auchmuty, on the left flank, held out in a strong position; but next day the situation was felt to be hopeless. Whitelocke came to terms with the Spaniards, and agreed to withdraw the British forces from the country. On his return to England, he too was tried by court-martial and cashiered. A popular toast for some time afterwards was 'success to grey hairs, but bad luck to white locks'.

The army left the River Plate in November; the 17th, spending their second Christmas in succession on board ship, arrived eventually at the regimental depot at Chichester in January 1808.

The fate of the two troops of 21st in the expedition is not known; there is evidence that one troop served in Madeira in 1808, and this troop must have come either from the Cape or from South America. The men of the 21st in the Cape were occupied in frontier duties, and in the protection of settlers' land against the natives whom they had evicted. A corps of Hottentots was formed to man

27

a chain of frontier posts, the ground in between being patrolled by cavalry. In 1812, a large force of soldiers and volunteer settlers attacked and drove out twenty thousand Kaffirs who had crossed the frontier and settled in the Zuurveld.

There were other troubles besides those caused by the Kaffirs; in 1815 a Dutch farmer named Bedizenhout refused to appear in court to answer to a charge of ill-treating a Hottentot; when British soldiers went to arrest him, he resisted, and was shot. His relations and friends swore to avenge him; a few days later a party of about four hundred surrounded a small British post and demanded its surrender. The Frontier Commandant, Colonel Cuyler, marched out against them at the head of a troop of the 21st. Thirty of the rebels surrendered, and the rest fled. They were pursued and about sixty were caught; the six leaders were tried, sentenced to death, and hanged in public at Schlachters Nek. The execution was particularly horrible, for the scaffold broke, and in a dreadful scene of confusion, with condemned men and spectators crying for mercy, the hanging had to be repeated a second time. At Schlachters Nek, as at the massacre of Waxhaws, the two regiments were to be involved in incidents which were to become bywords for colonial hatred of the British.

The 21st had two further duties in the southern hemisphere — the garrisoning of Tristan da Cunha in 1815 to prevent its use as a base for operations designed to rescue Napoleon from St. Helena; one troop formed part of the guard over the Emperor at St. Helena, and was present at his funeral in 1821. The rest of the Regiment sailed for England in 1817, and was disbanded on arrival at Chatham.

Chapter Five

The Conquest of India

THE MEN OF THE 17TH might be excused, had they arrived home in a poor state of morale. They were back from an unsuccessful campaign; they had been delayed by storms, and had spent their Christmas at sea; and now they were already under orders to sail for India within six weeks. Yet every man (but one, who was sick) reported punctually at the end of his leave, and the Mayor and Corporation of Chichester expressed their public gratitude – and amazement – at a regiment which could spend £3,000 in the town, without a single case of misbehaviour. Here was no 'uncontrouled licentiousness of a brutal and insolent soldiery'.

The 17th embarked for India under the command of Major Cotton (Lieutenant-Colonel Evan Lloyd being detained to give evidence at the court-martial of General Whitelocke, where no doubt he must have felt some satisfaction at being able to mention the mishandling of the cavalry). The convoy arrived in Calcutta in August; the voyage ended with the usual storms, and a fire in one of the ships. After a year in Calcutta, the regiment was transferred to the Bombay district, and was stationed at Surat, 200 miles north of Bombay. The regiment was well mounted, with two 'galloping guns' manned by its own soldiers, as part of the establishment.

In 1810, four troops, with some infantry, were sent to Mandavi, to put down a religious rising; there they fought a fierce little battle against fanatics armed with fourteen-foot spears. The 17th seem, perhaps rashly, to have preferred a hand-to-hand battle, rather than relying on their firearms and guns. All the officers were wounded, and three men killed, while the fanatics left 200 dead before they were finally dispersed.

One change in dress in 1810 must have been welcome to troops in India — 'clubs and queues are abolished in all ranks from this date, and the hair is in future to be cut close to the neck. No powder is to be used on duty'. No official tropical clothing was yet in use; white covers were worn over the shako, impractical successor to the helmet, otherwise the usual thick uniforms were worn. Only those who have experienced Indian hot weather will appreciate what this meant.

In 1815 the regiment crossed the Ran of Kutch in an expedition into the interior of the peninsula, where no British troops had been before. Another Oliver De Lancey, probably the Colonel's nephew, rode with the expedition, and was wounded. In 1817, war broke out in earnest, and the whole army in India was mobilized to surround and attack the Mahratta and Pindari forces — an alliance of warrior tribes in the plains of central India, based on the area roughly of the old southern Rajputana, with the headquarters of the leader in Sindhia, near Jhansi. The Pindaris were mobile, independent, and had to be hunted down to the last man. The campaign is difficult to follow, and impossible to summarize. The 17th, starting from Baroda in December 1817, spent three months in long forced marches, under extremes of temperature, until the temporary defeat of the Pindaris in March 1818. At the end of the year, fighting broke out again, but the movements of the 17th cannot be traced. Lieutenant-Colonel The Hon. Lincoln Stanhope, commanding the Regiment, received special mention in the campaign, and was given command of a force of brigade strength.

The 17th spent fourteen years in India; having arrived with a strength of 790 men, it lost during those years, 26 officers, and 796 men from cholera and other diseases; many others were wounded or killed in action. It received in India, as replacements, 929 of all ranks, and it sailed for England, in 1823, under 200 strong. We may wonder how many of those men who behaved so well in Chichester, and who had returned so punctually from their leave, ever saw their homes again?

On the way back, the ship carrying the remnants of the 17th touched at St. Helena. Here they learnt that General De Lancey had died in the previous autumn. He had been Colonel of the regiment for 28 years, and had fought in its very first action on Long Island nearly half a century earlier. For many years he had represented Maidstone in Parliament, and he died a bachelor in the home of his sister, Lady Dundas, wife of a Commander-in-Chief of the British Army.

The other interesting news that the 17th learnt at St. Helena, was that they were now a regiment of Lancers.

In 1816, the Duke of York, then Commander-in-Chief, had become interested in forming a corps of Lancers in imitation of the Polish cavalry who had fought with Napoleon. Fifty men of the 9th Light Dragoons were reviewed in the Queen's Riding House in Pimlico; they were dressed in blue and crimson, with grey trousers and blue cloth caps, and carried a lance sixteen feet long, with a red, white and blue pennon. Now five regiments were to be armed as lancers; carbines were handed into store (for sixty years), and the lance, obsolete even in Cromwell's day, became the principal weapon. It was to remain in use in war by the British cavalry for another century.

Lance drill was a hard (and rather dangerous) physical exercise, made even more difficult if the soldier was wearing the high and heavy lance cap, which in the Polish fashion, was to replace the shako. Uniforms of this period were extremely ornate − Fortescue wryly describes them as 'the zenith of expense, and the nadir of taste'. The wearing of moustaches was now made compulsory for all ranks.

When the 17th landed in England, one hundred and fifty of the survivors were invalided out, or discharged. Fortescue paints the picture of 250 new recruits, with bristly upper lips, being trained at Chatham in unfamiliar lance exercises, by the fifty remaining old soldiers. It is at such moments that tradition plays its part; how

31

else can a regiment be rebuilt by a handful of officers and men, unless they have the legends and the symbols and the standards of those who were there before? Men need these exemplars to help in working together; and reformers who from time to time have tried to abolish the regimental system have not succeeded in finding anything better to put in its place.

In 1826, Lieutenant-Colonel Stanhope was succeeded by George, Lord Bingham, better known later as Lord Lucan. Although also elected to Parliament in the same year, he was in fact a keen soldier, and joined the Russians in their war against the Turks in 1828, to gain experience of active service. He had served in five regiments before joining the 17th as a major; a year later he paid £25,000 for the appointment of Lieutenant-Colonel.

In receiving this appointment he forestalled another officer who had recently joined the 17th in the hope of getting command. This was Major Anthony Bacon, aged thirty, the outstanding British cavalry officer of his time. He had fought in the Peninsula with the 16th Light Dragoons and at Waterloo with the 10th Hussars. A keen student of tactics, he advocated the 'Rank Entire' system, which sought to abolish the use of two ranks in the charge – the second rank, he maintained, was only there to fall over the first.

Unfortunately, his patron, the Duke of York, died in 1827, and the 17th was given to Bingham. Bacon's father died soon afterwards, leaving the responsibility of the family estate in his hands. Bacon, a disappointed man, sent in his papers; later he went out to Portugal, where, in the war of 1832, he was able to prove his theories in practice with the Portuguese cavalry. He emerges briefly into the limelight in a pamphlet attacking Lord Lucan, after the latter's speech in the House of Lords, defending his conduct in the Crimea.

In twelve years of command Bingham spent fantastic sums in buying blood horses for all ranks, and in paying a fashionable tailor to make uniforms to his own designs. The 17th became known as 'Bingham's Dandies'. A year later, William IV came to the throne, and changed the whole army back into scarlet; he also ordered all moustaches to be shaved off again. These were years of pointless change and counter-change, for in 1840, Queen Victoria being on the throne, light dragoons and lancers returned to their blue uniforms. While the army seemed to go backwards in its development, in civilian life the Industrial Revolution was beginning. An incident at Birmingham gives us a vivid picture, symbolic of the declining power of the cavalry. A hundred men of the 17th, setting out on morning exercise, were approaching a bridge of the Liverpool railway line, when an engine, whistling loudly, passed rapidly overhead. Every horse stampeded; many men fell and were seriously injured, while the loose horses galloped madly back to barracks.

In this same year, 1843, HRH Prince George of Cambridge became Colonel of the Regiment, and later Colonel-in-Chief — an association which was to last till 1904.

In the next ten years the 17th served in England and Ireland; putting down riots in Leeds; parading before the Czar at Windsor; putting down more riots in Ireland; and escorting Queen Victoria into Dublin. At last, after thirty-four years of peace, orders came to prepare once again for active service. This time, the enemy was Russia.

Chapter Six

The Crimean War

GEORGE BINGHAM HAD relinquished command of the 17th in 1837; the regiment gave him a send-off which indicated that at his retirement from command he was popular with all ranks, although ten years before, when he first came to the regiment, he had earned the reputation of being a harsh martinet. Now, seventeen years after his retirement on half-pay, he offered his services to the Commander-in-Chief, Lord Hardinge, hoping that his previous experience in the Balkans might fit him for the command of an infantry brigade. His brother-in-law, James Brudenell, Earl of Cardigan, whom he detested, similarly applied to Lord Raglan, the newly appointed Commander-in-Chief of the Expeditionary Force. Lord Cardigan's name was a by-word for intolerance and oppression; he had been removed from command of the 15th Hussars for his persecution of one of his captains; his conduct of affairs in the 11th Hussars had created a national scandal; only the support of the Duke of Wellington and the Queen had prevented another removal from command.

It seems incredible now that these two men, aged 54 and 57, were both given high commands – to Lord Lucan, the whole Cavalry Division, to Lord Cardigan the Light Brigade; and the Heavy Brigade went to Colonel James Scarlett, aged 55. Only Lord Lucan had seen active service. These appointments were the result of a system exercised by the Duke of Wellington, who held that

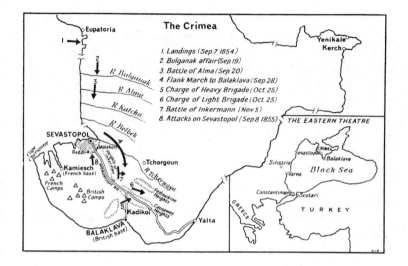

The Crimea

1. Landings (Sep 7 1854)
2. Bulganak affair (Sep 19)
3. Battle of Alma (Sep 20)
4. Flank March to Balaklava (Sep 28)
5. Charge of Heavy Brigade (Oct 25)
6. Charge of Light Brigade (Oct 25)
7. Battle of Inkermann (Nov 5)
8. Attacks on Sevastopol (Sep 8 1855)

THE EASTERN THEATRE

higher command in the Army was the prerogative of the aristocracy; regimental officers, such as Anthony Bacon, however experienced, were passed over. Although many of them had spent years of active service in the east, their talents were ignored, and they were slightingly dubbed 'Indian officers'. The soldiers may have wondered that if men of such dubious qualifications were to be appointed to the command of the fighting formations, what sort of officers might be found in charge of the less glamorous task of administration? They were soon to find out.

The war between Russia and Turkey had flared up, on the pretext, chosen by the Czar, of a dispute in Jerusalem between Russian Orthodox and Roman Catholic monks. In the ensuing riots, some Orthodox monks were killed; the Czar accused the Turkish police of allowing the Orthodox monks to be murdered, and invaded the Turkish provinces on the Danube.

Russia, from her great naval base at Sebastopol in the Crimea, had attacked and defeated the Turkish fleet at Sinope in the Black Sea. The British government, frightened by the appearance of their traditional bogey — a Russian fleet in the Mediterranean

— declared war. Napoleon III of France joined in, as much from a desire to achieve a military success as for any other reason.

The 17th sailed in April 1854, and arrived at Kulali on the Bosphorus in May. A few days later the regiment embarked again for Varna in Bulgaria. Lord Cardigan (without consulting his divisional commander, Lord Lucan) applied to Lord Raglan to embark his staff at the same time, and the Light Brigade was formed up at Varna. Conditions were bad, forage and water were short, and cholera soon broke out. In mid-May Lord Raglan arrived in Varna, where the objective was the relief of the Turkish town of Silistria, 80 miles inland on the Danube, besieged by the Russians.

In June the Heavy Brigade arrived in Varna, but still the army made no move. Lord Lucan was still left behind at Kulali, and to his indignation, Lord Cardigan took command of the whole cavalry division in Varna. By the time Lord Lucan arrived in Varna, the Light Brigade was eight miles inland at Devna. His Lordship had to be content with drilling the Heavy Brigade, at which exercise he proved himself completely out of date. On June 15, the Turks, unaided by British or French troops, raised the siege of Silistria. Lord Raglan ordered a cavalry reconnaissance to the banks of the Danube; Lord Cardigan took two hundred men of the Light Brigade on this patrol, which resulted in the death of nearly a hundred horses. The 17th, fortunately for them, did not take part. In July, Lord Cardigan took the Light Brigade into camp on a hot desert plateau, thirty miles inland, called Yeni-Bazaar, where the troops were bored and depressed by inactivity.

In July also, Lord Raglan decided to invade the Crimea, in order to destroy Sebastopol, and to put an end to the Russian threat to the Mediterranean.

The Cavalry Division embarked on September 2; Lord Lucan, its commander, had once again been ordered to stay behind, but this time he insisted on his right to embark with his command. The expedition sailed, without a landing place having yet been selected! Lord Raglan's steamer went on ahead of the expedition, and the Commander-in-Chief with his staff, including the

Quartermaster-General, Richard Airey, made a personal reconnaissance of the coast, and chose a beach near Eupatoria, called Calamita Bay.

The beach in fact was ideal; the landing, at 6 a.m. on September 14, was unopposed, and, under the management of the Royal Navy, was very efficiently carried out. Seven battalions of the Light Division were put on shore in the first hour, and 14,000 British troops were landed by 3 p.m. The French, who throughout the campaign were rather more efficient than the British, put 6,000 men ashore in 22 minutes. The next three days were spent in landing the cavalry, artillery and stores. For transport, 350 carts were seized from the local inhabitants. The British were without tents and when the weather broke on the first night, were soaked to the skin; the French soldiers had a small 'dog tent' each, which kept them dry.

Gradually the confusion increased; cholera continued to take a steady toll from the ranks; stores piled up on the beach; the cavalry, who should have been reconnoitring inland, waited in vain for orders from Lord Raglan. At last, on September 9, the army marched southwards. In front, the 11th and 18th Hussars under Lord Cardigan formed the advance guard. On the right, against the sea, marched the French and the Turks; next on the landward side came a column composed of the 2nd and 3rd Infantry Divisions; on their left again, the Light Division and the 1st Division of Guards and Highlanders commanded by the Duke of Cambridge; on the left, as flank guard, were the 8th Hussars and the 17th Lancers, under Lord Lucan; as rearguard, the 4th Light Dragoons. The 4th Division stayed in the beach-head to protect the stores.

In the early afternoon, when the infantry were already suffering tortures from heat and thirst, the four squadrons of the advance guard, crossing the valley of the River Bulganek, sighted a detachment of Cossacks on the opposite slope. Lord Raglan, still on the higher ground behind, saw that beyond the Cossacks was the Russian main force of cavalry, and behind them again, a huge body of infantry and guns. Unwilling to risk a battle on unfavourable ground, with his troops exhausted by the heat, Lord Raglan recalled the advance guard, much to their disgust. The Russians fired a few shots at long range, and withdrew southwards. The army bivouacked for the night, continuing the march next morning to the River Alma.

Here the Russians expected to destroy the Allied armies, for beyond the meadows and the river, rose the heights, a steep bare slope, 500 to 700 feet high, crowned with earthworks, containing 100 guns and 40,000 men, with the Russian cavalry guarding their landward flank. The plan was for the French and Turks to cross the river on the right, supported by the guns of the fleet; once the river crossing was secured, the British were to attack on the centre and left.

The cavalry sat through the day, awaiting the charge of the Russian cavalry (which never came), while wave after wave of infantry assaulted the heights. Eventually Lord Lucan lost patience and led some of the cavalry, including the 17th, up to the heights beside Sir Colin Campbell's Highlanders. The enemy were by now on the run, and the British cavalry should have been able to complete their destruction. But the handling of cavalry was not Lord Raglan's *forte*; orders came that the cavalry were to escort the guns, and on no account to pursue the enemy. Once more they felt themselves humiliated; Captain Nolan, of the 15th Hussars, ADC to General Airey, said to William Russell, correspondent of *The Times*, 'there were one thousand British cavalry, looking on at a beaten army retreating…it is enough to drive one mad!'

The army bivouacked again, among the dreadful litter of the battlefield, and two days later marched round the flank of the city of Sebastopol. The cavalry advance guard got lost in thick scrub country, and Lord Raglan and his staff ran into the rearguard of the retreating Russians. He sent a staff officer to find the cavalry; eventually Lord Lucan was located and directed towards the enemy; a few prisoners and wagons were taken, but pursuit was again forbidden. The Allies now crossed the River Tchernaya, and arrived on the coast south of Sebastopol; the French occupying Kamiesh as their base, while the British took the land-locked harbour of Balaclava. An early attack on Sebastopol would almost certainly have succeeded; but the Allies waited until their heavy artillery was in position, by which time the brilliant German-Russian engineer Todleben had put the defences into such good order, that Sebastopol was to hold out for twelve months more. The Allies invested Sebastopol from the landward side; their camps lay on the high bare plateau of the Chersonese. The French were near to their base at Kamiesh, while the British were nine miles from Balaclava. Their supplies came up through the hills by a rutted road, which ran first through a gorge, guarded by a little hill at Kadikoi; from there the road traversed a long ridge of hills running east and west in the Balaclava plain, called the Causeway Heights; finally the road wound through a gorge in the Heights of Inkerman on to the plateau. The Woronzoff Road, as it was called, was the lifeline of the British forces. The main body of the British infantry was encamped around Sebastopol. Sir Colin Campbell's 93rd Argyll and Sutherland Highlanders were posted on the hill at Kadikoi, as outposts of the Balaclava garrison. North of Kadikoi, at the foot of the Causeway Heights, lay the cavalry camp. On the Causeway Heights were six redoubts, numbered from east to west, manned by Turkish troops, and armed with twelve-pounder guns and crews from the Navy.

The Russian army outside Sebastopol was based at Tchorgoun, north of the River Tchernaya. The 17th took part in patrolling daily to the river, to watch for any signs of enemy activity, and in mid-October Captain White observed a large body of Russian cavalry on the move. The weather was getting colder now, and on the morning of October 23 news came that 20,000 infantry and 5,000 cavalry were advancing on Balaclava. The 4th Infantry Division was hastily sent down from the heights, while Lord Lucan ordered the cavalry to stand-to. They were kept at readiness from 5 p.m. to 7 a.m. in the bitter cold; Major Willett, commanding the 17th, died of exposure in the night. The next senior officer, Captain William Morris, who was on the staff, returned immediately to take command of the regiment. Morris, an 'Indian officer' of great experience, was very popular with the regiment, and was a great friend of Nolan of the 15th. At dawn on the 24th there was no sign of the Russians; the 4th Division returned to the heights and the cavalry stood down.

On the 25th, Lord Lucan set out on his usual morning inspection of the front; the cavalry had stood-to an hour before daylight in accordance with his orders. As he approached No. 1 Redoubt at the east of the Causeway Heights, he saw that two flags were flying from its signal mast — 'enemy in sight!' At that moment the guns in the redoubt opened fire. Lord George Paget of the 4th Light Dragoons was temporarily in command of the Light Brigade, as it was too early in the day for Lord Cardigan (who was still at breakfast on his yacht). Lord George was sent at full gallop to warn the Cavalry Division to mount; and an ADC was despatched to Lord Raglan (at his morning reconnaissance on the heights of Inkerman) to tell him that 11,000 Russian infantry were advancing on the Causeway Heights. Lord Lucan led out the Heavy Brigade to see whether a feint would slow the Russian advance, but the packed masses of Russian infantry ignored the British threat, and moved steadily towards the redoubts.

Lord Lucan therefore withdrew to the south slopes at the west end of the Causeway Heights. Here he was in touch with Sir Colin Campbell, and excellently placed to threaten the flank of any force advancing from the Causeway Heights towards Kadikoi and Balaclava. Lord Lucan's conduct of affairs so far had been faultless — his unpopular 'stand-to' had proved its value; his tactical moves had been intelligent and sound.

Above on the heights Lord Raglan, with General Canrobert, the French Commander, ordered the French cavalry into a position immediately below him at the west end of the North Valley — a long open valley bounded on the south by Causeway Heights, and on the north by the Fedioukine Heights. Lord Raglan then, to Lord Lucan's fury and dismay, ordered the Light Brigade to return from their position in support of Sir Colin Campbell, and to 'take ground to the left of the second line of redoubts'.

The Russians, seeing the removal of the Light Brigade covering Kadikoi, detached four squadrons and directed them on to the Highlanders, followed by the main body of some 3,000 strong.

Lord Raglan reacted at last, and sent his second order to Lord Lucan — 'eight squadrons of Heavy Dragoons to be detached towards Balaclava to support the Turks, who are wavering'. Indeed the Turks had abandoned Redoubts 2, 3 and 4, when No. 1 had fallen after a stiff fight. The first four squadrons of Russian cavalry bore down on the Highlanders, who rose from the ground in a 'thin red line' two deep, and drove the Russians back by deadly accurate rifle fire. General Scarlett's Heavy Brigade, hurrying to the support of the Highlanders, suddenly saw the main body of the Russian cavalry coming over the top of the Causeway Heights. The Heavy Brigade wheeled left into line and charged uphill at a jog trot, among the tents and picket lines of their own camp. The four hundred British were swallowed up in the immense grey mass of Russians. The Inniskillings and Greys were in the lead; the 4th Dragoon Guards fell on the Russian right flank, and the 5th Dragoon Guards and the Royals followed them. To the delight of the spectators, the Russian cavalry wavered and began to break.

Half a mile away, on the flank, the Light Brigade sat watching. Captain Godfrey Morgan[1] of the 17th wrote 'we saw all, sitting still, our swords tightly grasped in our hands, and our spurs at our horses' sides, burning to be let loose upon them; but the order came not....' The order did not come from Lord Raglan, who wished to keep his cavalry in hand until two infantry divisions had come down from the heights; the order did not come from Lord Cardigan, who had been put into the position by Lord Lucan, and therefore considered it to be his duty to stay there; the order did not come from Lord Lucan, who believed that he had told Lord Cardigan to attack anything within reach of the position. Captain Morris of the 17th boldly rode out and asked Lord Cardigan if he could charge with the 17th. Private Wightman heard Lord Cardigan reply 'No, no, sir' and Morris, returning to his post say, 'My God, my God, what a chance we are losing.' The Russian cavalry, unmolested, withdrew across the Causeway Heights, and took up a position, behind their guns, at the east end of the North Valley. The British

[1] (Later 1st Viscount Tredegar)

41

infantry now began to arrive, so Lord Raglan sent his third order to Lord Lucan: 'Cavalry to advance and take advantage of any opportunity to recover the heights. They will be supported by infantry which have been ordered to advance on two fronts.' Lord Lucan received the last part of this message as 'They will be supported by infantry which have been ordered. Advance on two fronts' and he read it to mean that he must wait for the infantry; so he moved the Light Brigade to the west end of the north valley, and waited. From this position, he could not see the Causeway Heights, where now Russian artillery teams appeared, with rope tackles to drag away the guns from the redoubts. Lord Raglan on the heights above, called for General Airey and dictated his fourth order: 'Lord Raglan wishes the cavalry to advance rapidly to the front, follow the enemy, and try to prevent the enemy carrying away the guns. Troop Horse Artillery may accompany. French cavalry is on your left. Immediate.'

Airey signed the order, and handed it to an ADC, but Lord Cardigan said 'Send Nolan' and to Nolan 'tell Lord Lucan the cavalry is to attack immediately.'

Nolan was a superb horseman, the author of two works on training cavalry horses. He galloped headlong down the heights, with the order for Lord 'Look-on' the old man whom he felt to be responsible for the humiliating inaction of the light cavalry. When Nolan got down into the valley, the redoubts were no longer visible. While Lord Lucan read the order, Nolan angrily repeated Lord Raglan's message – 'Attack? Attack what? What guns, sir?' said Lord Lucan. Nolan pointed vaguely to the head of the valley and replied, 'There, my Lord, is your enemy, there are your guns,' and in this moment signed the death warrant of the Light Brigade. Having delivered his message, he rode over to his friend Morris, determined to join in the charge with the 17th.

Lord Lucan now ordered Lord Cardigan to advance with the Light Brigade, while he followed with the Heavy Brigade. Lord Cardigan actually queried the sense of the order, but Lord Lucan said that there was no choice but to obey. Lord Cardigan rode back, saying, 'Well, here goes the last of the Brudenells.' He ordered the

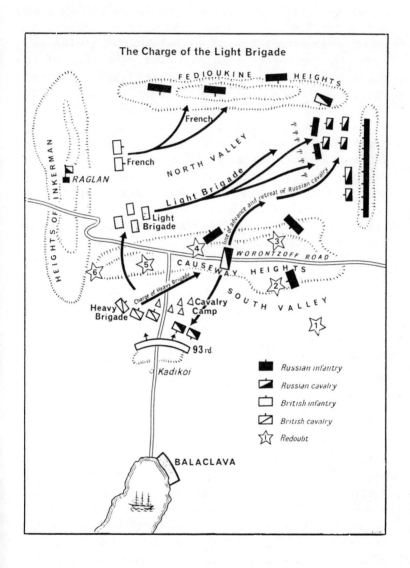

The Charge of the Light Brigade

FEDIOUKINE HEIGHTS

HEIGHTS OF INKERMAN

French

French

RAGLAN

NORTH VALLEY

Light Brigade

Light Brigade

line of advance and retreat of Russian cavalry

WORONTZOFF ROAD

CAUSEWAY HEIGHTS

SOUTH VALLEY

Charge of Heavy Brigade

Heavy Brigade

Cavalry Camp

93rd.

Kadikoi

Russian infantry

Russian cavalry

British infantry

British cavalry

Redoubt

BALACLAVA

43

Brigade into two lines; in the first the 13th Light Dragoons, 11th Hussars and 17th Lancers, in the second the 4th Light Dragoons and the 8th Hussars. Lord Lucan however ordered the 11th into the second line, as he felt the valley to be too narrow. The alteration further annoyed Lord Cardigan, since it was his own regiment that was being displaced. The 17th was therefore on the left of the front line, 139 men strong, with two squadrons in line commanded by Captains White and Winter. Just before the advance began, they were joined by the Regimental butcher, Veigh, with a heavy dragoon's equipment worn over his bloodstained canvas smock, and carrying his pole-axe instead of a lance.

Led by Lord Cardigan, the Brigade rode steadily on at the trot, when suddenly Nolan, leaving the 17th, galloped across the front to Lord Cardigan, waving his sword. Morris called out, 'No, no, Nolan! That won't do, we have a long way to go and must be steady,' when a shell burst near Lord Cardigan, and a fragment hit Nolan in the heart. His horse trotted back through the 4th Light Dragoons, with Nolan screaming in pain, until he fell from the saddle.

Sergeant-Major Nunnerly, riding with the right-hand squadron of the 17th, considered that Nolan actually shouted 'Threes right' — which would have changed the direction of the advance completely. Nolan's horse swung to the right, and part of the squadron started to follow him. Nunnerly called out 'Front forward' and brought them into line again. He himself survived the charge. His medals were recently acquired by the Regiment.

Lord Cardigan was horrified at Nolan's irregular action, and afterwards said to General Scarlett 'imagine the fellow screaming like a woman when he was hit.' But it seems certain that Nolan had in fact realized his mistake, and that he was trying to draw Lord Cardigan's attention to the redoubts on the Causeway Heights; and that there was despair as well as pain in his death-cry.

The Brigade rode on in perfect order, with but one command continually repeated, 'Close up, close up' as the dwindling lines advanced. The 17th squadron on the right broke into a canter, but Lord Cardigan laid his sword across the chest of Captain White, and told him to keep in line. Still, the ranks advanced in perfect order, and General Bosquet looking on from the heights exclaimed in horror 'C'est magnifique, mais ce n'est pas la guerre.' As the Light Brigade vanished into the smoke of the Russian guns, the French commander sent the Chasseurs d'Afrique to attack the Russian batteries on the Fedioukine Heights; the charge was a brilliant success, and the enemy fire on that flank was silenced.

Lord Lucan, following with the Heavy Brigade, decided that he could not risk its destruction, and decided to halt and 'protect the Light Cavalry against pursuit on their return'.

The Light Brigade received a full salvo from the Russian guns at a range of eighty yards. Lord Cardigan miraculously survived, and passed through the line of guns, coming face to face with the Russian cavalry beyond. A Russian officer recognized him, and tried to take him alive, but he escaped, and rode quietly back down the valley alone.

William Morris also reached the Russian cavalry, and ran a Russian officer through with his sword; tethered by his sword arm to the corpse, he was wounded and forced to surrender; he escaped, was dragged by a spare horse which he tried to catch, mounted another which was shot under him, and eventually was rescued under fire by Corporal Charles Wooden of the 17th, and Doctor James Mouat, surgeon of the 6th Dragoons, who were both awarded the Victoria Cross for their bravery.

The Victoria Cross was also awarded to Sergeants John Berryman and John Farrell of the 17th, for protecting Captain Webb, who was badly wounded. Although ordered by their officer to leave him, they carried him as far as they could out of range of the enemy guns.

The Light Brigade set about the crews of the Russian battery, and then turned on the cavalry who stood behind the guns. Lord Cardigan's Brigade Major, Major Mayow, rallied the remnants of the 17th and 13th, and charged a Russian squadron advancing on the guns; 70 survivors of the 4th and 11th fought their way out under the leadership of Lord George Paget; the 8th Hussars joined with Mayow's little group, and cut their way through yet another Russian squadron standing in the way of retreat. So the little groups of men made their way painfully back down the North Valley; some Russian lancers attempting to cut them off, were fired on by mistake by their own infantry and guns, and withdrew. Of 700 men who had ridden in the charge, 195 returned. The 17th was reduced to a strength of three officers and 35 men. While the Light Brigade reformed on the Causeway Heights, the two infantry divisions and the Heavy Brigade expected to attack the redoubts; Lord Raglan was in favour of an attack, but General Canrobert was strongly against it, and the battle died out at about 4 p.m.

The Russians were allowed to keep the three eastern redoubts, which dominated the Woronzoff road. The battle was felt to be a draw; Balaclava was safe, though the redoubts were gone. But the loss of the road meant that the army in the camps was to suffer untold hardship in the coming winter.

On November 5 the Russians attacked the Heights of Inkerman, in an attempt to relieve Sebastopol; the cavalry took little part; the 17th stood under heavy fire, in reserve behind the Guards, receiving many casualties to both men and horses.

On November 14 a hurricane wrecked the harbour; many ships were sunk, and stores were lost or ruined. Sergeant-Major Nunnerly tells how a soldier of the 17th, knowing his wife was on board one of the ships, and that she had all their savings round her waist in a money-belt, went down to the beach in the hopes of finding her. Amongst the wreckage and debris of the storm, he found her dead body, with the money belt intact beneath her corsets.

Conditions in the camps now went from bad to worse; the horses were starving, eating each others' tails, and dying in the lines. Incompetence and apathy spread through the army. Ships full of grain sailed in and sailed away again without being unloaded; stores lay in the mud unopened, while the troops starved; plague, cholera and dysentery swept through the ranks; the British Army seemed to have lost all heart.

In many regiments the officers had not been trained to think about the welfare of the men. Garnet Wolseley, then a subaltern of infantry, wrote scathingly of the young man of the Light Brigade who, though brave and dashing, had little idea of the mere mundane duties of a regimental officer. The example set by their Brigadier, living in comfort on his yacht, was not calculated to improve their 'man management'.

The winter of 1854 was perhaps the lowest point ever reached in administration in the British Army. The public outcry which ensued from the reports of newspaper correspondents, and from the letters written home by officers and men in the field, stimulated a drive to improve administration which resulted in the evolution of better techniques in organization, transport, medical work, and catering, which laid the foundation for nearly all the present-day administrative services.

The 17th received drafts of men and horses, enough to enable them to take part in patrol and foraging duties in the summer of 1855 and in the battles of Tchernaya and Sebastopol. The Russians evacuated Sebastopol in September and the war faded out in the spring of 1856. The 17th left Balaclava in November 1855 for Ismid on the Bosphorus, and sailed again for Ireland in May; there it was quartered at Clogheen, Clonmel, Fethard and Limerick, moving later in the year to Dublin.

Chapter Seven

The Indian Mutiny

THE INDIAN MUTINY broke out at Meerut in May 1857; the 17th sailed from England in October, arrived in India in December, and was posted to Kirkee. Lieutenant-Colonel Benson, with the Riding-Master, the Veterinary Surgeon, and four roughriders, had travelled ahead by the overland route in order to make arrangements for the issue of horses from the remount depot in Bombay. It was not until May 1858 that the first squadron of the 17th, under Sir William Gordon, was ready for service. By this time the mutiny was nearly over, except that in the Malwa, in Central India, the rebels' most talented leader, Tantia Topi, was still at large. He was the friend and confidant of the Nana Sahib, Maharaja of Bithur, whose dream it was to re-establish the Mahratta Empire at the expense of the British. But now Tantia Topi was on the run; he had been defeated by Sir Colin Campbell at Cawnpore, by Sir Hugh Rose at Jhansi, Kunch and Gwalior and was now heading westwards for Tonk.

The 17th was returning to the scenes of the Pindari War fifty years earlier. Sir William Gordon's squadron was ordered to march from Kirkee to Mhow. Early in the journey, the *babu* in charge of the commissariat deserted, his duty being taken over by young Evelyn Wood, who as a midshipman had watched the Crimean expedition landing at 'Calamity Bay'. He had transferred to the 13th Hussars in 1855, and thence to the 17th. He was the only officer in the regiment who could speak Hindustani.

Sir William Gordon had fought with great courage at Balaclava, receiving five sabre wounds in the head. Much has been written about the inefficiency and bad administration of cavalry officers in the Crimea; if Sir William Gordon was an example of the training officers in the 17th, then the regiment had nothing to fear from critics of the cavalry. His squadron marched the 500 miles from Kirkee to Mhow without a day's halt, arriving without a single sore back. Sir William's custom was to inspect each horse at the end of the day's march, adjusting the stuffing of the saddle, if necessary, with a two-pronged fork. If there was any sign of soreness, the rider could look forward to walking on his feet until the back was cured. General Michel, whose column the 17th were to join, wrote, in a glowing report on Gordon and his squadron at the end of the campaign:

> ...this officer's care was extended to the comfort of his men, the care of baggage animals, and even to the well-being of camp followers...the general system of the regiment is one which must lead to efficiency; but this squadron has come so repeatedly under his observation in action and otherwise, that he [*the General*] cannot let it depart without specially recording his observation of its merits.

Michel's column pursued Tantia Topi in the full heat of the Indian summer, eventually catching him at Mangrauli, where the small British force of 90 cavalry, 1,000 infantry and four guns, defeated 5,000 rebels and six guns. Tantia fled east across the Betwa; Michel overtook him at Sindhwa, where Evelyn Wood won the Victoria Cross, attacking single-handed a squadron of mutineers from the Bengal Infantry.

The pursuit of Tantia Topi lasted for nine months, and covered more than a thousand miles. Two more squadrons of the 17th arrived at Mhow in September, and joined Michel's column in the hunt at Hoshangabad in November. On January 1, 1859, the remaining squadron, which had been in the south at Sholapur, joined Brigadier Somerset's column, and after an approach march of 147 miles took part at Baroda in a brilliant charge against 5,000 native cavalry. The battle of Baroda finally dispersed Tantia's forces. His supporters left him; he fled northwards across the Banas River, pursued by Somerset's column, which covered 230 miles in six days and a half. The enemy's horses foundered at the pace; three hundred of Tantia's supporters surrendered without a fight, and Tantia himself took to the jungle, until he was betrayed to the British in April, tried by court-martial and hanged. The farrier-sergeant of the 17th assisted at the hanging, and took the rope as a souvenir.

The 17th remained in Central India for a year, and then marched south to Secunderabad, losing on the way (from cholera) Veigh, the Balaclava butcher. William Morris, who had led the charge, also died in India during this campaign. After five quiet years in Secunderabad, the 17th returned to England in 1865.

In 1857, when the government of India was assumed by the Crown, five regiments of European cavalry which had been raised by the East India Company, were transferred to the Queen's service. The 3rd Bengal Light Cavalry became the 21st Light Dragoons, then in 1863 the title was changed to 21st Hussars. The recruits, raised in England and trained at Warley in Hampshire, were below the usual standard of height, so the 21st received the charming nickname of 'The Dumpies'. The 21st stayed in Bengal until 1873, and then moved to England.

Chapter Eight

The Zulu War and the Sudan

THE 17TH AND 21ST, now home in England, had been in existence for just over a century, the 17th in unbroken span, the 21st in several periods totalling a little over thirty years of embodiment, and as yet, bearing no battle honours. A current joke about the 21st was that their motto was 'Thou shalt not kill' − but it was not the fault of the Regiment that they had as yet seen little active service − their turn was soon to come.

The 17th had surely been into more odd corners of the world than any other regiment in the army. From the Ran of Kutch to the River Plate, from South Carolina to Nova Scotia, from San Domingo to Persepolis (where in 1810 Sergeant Willock and Private Cloyne had carved their names and the motto upon the walls of Xerxes' palace) − the men of the 17th had fought, or died, or gone upon their various duties. The only place in which the Death's Head had hardly been seen was in the great European theatres of Spain, France and Belgium, in the wars against Napoleon. The 17th's role in the wars in America, and in India against the Pindaris and Tantia Topi, had been true cavalry actions, of reconnaissance, manoeuvre and pursuit; in the Crimea they had been handled − and mishandled − in the Napoleonic manner of cavalry as a massed, mobile, shock weapon. Everywhere else, they had played their part as mounted or dismounted infantry, as the occasion demanded. The history of British regular cavalry tactics had been, and was to

51

remain, a matter of great uncertainty. The argument was, at heart, between those at one extreme who visualized the cavalry as mounted infantry and at the other those who preferred shock action with the 'arme blanche'. Within these two main divisions lay other, more subtle causes, each championed keenly by its exponents — rifle or carbine — lance or sword — cutting or thrusting. Far too much time and thought was expended upon these details, and upon matters of dress, rather than upon a clear policy of the correct role of the cavalry. When such a policy did appear, the cavalry seldom carried it out in practice, preferring at the slightest opportunity to charge at the gallop, regardless of the consequences. Now and again a cavalry leader of talent emerged, who was capable not only of devising effectual tactics for his horsemen, but also of controlling them in the necessary manoeuvres; but for every genius there were scores of leaders with neither ability nor interest in their profession.

The 17th had been fortunate in being so much abroad, since foreign service ensured a good proportion of officers with battle experience. Long periods of home service tended — and still tends — to drive the 'professional' soldiers to despair with boredom, while at the same time attracting the 'playboys' who are looking for the opportunities for a sporting life. Perhaps the best — or worst — example of this type of officer was Beau Brummell, who after a short period as an officer in the 10th Hussars, is said to have resigned because he could not face 'foreign service' when the regiment was posted to Manchester! The 17th, in the years of doldrums before the Crimea, had been commanded by one 'fashionable' officer — the Earl of Lucan — but he had been a keen soldier, and had demanded the highest standards that he knew. His successors have all been regimental officers with long service in the 17th.

After the Crimea, Lord Lucan was eventually promoted to Field-Marshal — (the first of five to whom the 17th can lay claim) — and died in 1888. The Duke of Cambridge, who had commanded — and personally led — the 1st Division in the Crimea, became Commander-in-Chief of the Army in 1856, and held the appointment for no less than 39 years, during which time the army

The engagement of the River Bulganek. The 17th Lancers wait below the Staff. On the right the Royal Horse Artillery deploy behind the advance guard, while the enemy guns fire the opening rounds of the Crimean War.

Balaclava — a contemporary engraving of the Charge from the Fedioukine Heights. Far centre, Balaclava Harbour, far right the Heavy Brigade — beyond the charge, the line of redoubts. The 17th are on the left of the front rank.

An officer of the 17th Lancers, by Henry Barraud. This portrait
was painted between 1859 and 1869; in the appendix on dress at the
end of this book the reader can find a key describing all the details
of dress and saddlery in this picture.

Portrait in the possession of the Regiment

The Zulu War — The 17th wait in the square at Ulundi, before
going out to charge the Zulu impis.

From the Graphic

Private Thomas Byrne, one of the three 21st Lancers awarded the VC at Omdurman.

The Battle of Omdurman — the final phase. Beyond the Djebel Surgham, the 21st Lancers charge into a somewhat exaggerated mass of Dervishes guarding the retreat of the main body towards Omdurman.

The cavalry wait — saddled up and ready to move during the Arras offensive, April 1917.

Imperial War Museum

The cavalry go through — advancing during the Arras offensive in 1917. In the foreground infantry occupy a shattered German trench; in the background a belt of wire strangles movement through the sea of mud. Top centre, a stranded tank.

Imperial War Museum

was to be very greatly reformed. Purchase and sale of commissions were abolished; the 'short service system' (six years with the colours and six with the reserve) was introduced; flogging was abolished; the carbine was brought back for the cavalry; uniforms were improved and simplified. The Duke of Cambridge was promoted Field-Marshal in 1862, and appointed Colonel-in-Chief of the 17th in 1877 − from which date the regiment bore the title 'Duke of Cambridge's Own'.

For the 17th and the 21st, the next theatre of war was to be the continent of Africa − for the 17th, Zululand and the Boer War, for the 21st Egypt and the Sudan.

In 1879, war broke out with the Zulus over disputes about the boundaries of their territory and the Transvaal, annexed by Great Britain in 1877. Although a boundary commission found in favour of the Zulus, Sir Bartle Frere, the High Commissioner, was convinced that the Zulu leader Cetewayo, should be controlled. The ultimatum demanding compensation for the frontier incidents, and laying down the future structure of Zululand was rejected; in January 1879 a British force invaded Zululand. Lord Chelmsford, the commander, had 5,000 Europeans and 8,000 natives, against 40,000 Zulus. The force crossed the frontier in three columns, converging on the royal kraal at Ulundi. The centre column was surprised by 10,000 Zulus at Isandlwhana, overwhelmed and destroyed on January 22. Two *impis* of the Zulu army advanced on Rorke's Drift, where they were only repulsed after a protracted defence by a very small force.

Reinforcements, including the 17th Lancers, were hastily embarked in England, arriving in the Rorke's Drift area in May.

The British forces were content to hold their ground during March and April; one column under Colonel Pearson was besieged at Eshowe, while the other under Colonel Evelyn Wood defeated the best troops of Cetewayo's army at Kambula.

In July, Lord Chelmsford returned to the offensive, the objective once more being the royal kraal at Ulundi. On July 4 the 2nd Division, under Major-General Marshall, crossed the White Umvolosi River, and advanced on the kraal, the 17th forming the divisional rear-guard. The column was surrounded by a huge force of Zulus; the infantry formed hollow square, with the cavalry standing-by in the centre. The Zulu attack, which began at 8.50 a.m., was continued for three-quarters of an hour, against heavy rifle and artillery fire. At 9.30 the Zulus began to waver and General Marshall ordered the 17th to attack. The regiment rode out of the square, formed echelon of wings, rank entire, on a front of 300 yards, and charged. The Zulus were concealed in long grass, from which came a hot fire; the 17th charged right through them; the Zulus scattered and ran, while the 17th pursued for two miles with the lance. The Zulu army was defeated and dispersed, never taking the field again.

The 17th lost two officers and one man killed, three officers and five men wounded and 26 horses killed or wounded.

After the Zulu War the 17th left Africa for India, but did not take part in the Afghan War, since the saddlery which was issued in Mhow proved to be so defective that the regiment, from no fault of its own, was not fit for active service. After nine years of uneventful service, the regiment returned to England.

Meanwhile, the attention of all Britain was directed on the fate of one man – General Charles George Gordon, the Governor-General of the Sudan, who was besieged in Khartoum by the forces of Mohammed Ahmed Ibn Seyid Abdullah, who had proclaimed himself as the Mahdi, and had raised the tribes against British-Egyptian rule. In March 1884, the tribes north of Khartoum blocked all traffic on the Nile; the telegraph was cut, and all communication with Khartoum ceased. Gordon had no British troops with him; his force consisted of 8,000 native soldiers, and five armed steamers. After six months' vacillation, the British Government formed the 'Gordon Relief Expedition'; this force, specially designed for the occasion, was to consist of four regiments of a Camel Corps to operate across the desert, and a strong column of infantry to work their way up the Nile in boats. Two regiments of the Camel Corps were formed from the cavalry, one from the Guards, and one from the infantry of the line. The 21st Hussars sent Major W. G. Crole-Wyndham, Lieutenant Fowle and 43 soldiers, to join the Light Camel Regiment. The Desert Column, some 2,000 strong, was to strike across country from Korti to Metemma. They were met by 10,000 Dervishes near the wells of Abu Klea, and after one of the bloodiest actions ever fought in the Sudan, the Camel Corps encamped at the wells; it was vital to them to reach the river at Metemma, since the force was desperately short of water. Leaving half the force to guard the wounded and baggage, a small square of 900 men fought their way twenty-five miles to the safety of the river through the Dervish army. Gordon's four steamers arrived to meet the Desert Column, but there was a delay of three days in starting for Khartoum, during which time the Mahdi's forces attacked Khartoum, overran the town, and killed Gordon.

The withdrawal of the Camel Corps was as difficult as its advance, but the expedition eventually reached Dongola, and when the Sudan was evacuated in May, the Camel Corps was disbanded.

The 21st Hussars went to India in 1888, returning to Egypt in 1896. In the following year, as the 21st Lancers, the regiment was to provide the British cavalry element in a force which set out to reconquer the Sudan.

By the time the 21st arrived, communications up the Nile had been opened by the construction, with enormous difficulty, of a desert railway from Wadi Halfa, across the loop of the river, to Abu Hamed, and to Atbara; thence the Nile was navigable as far as the 6th Cataract, above Metemma. The first duty of the 21st was to escort the artillery horses, the transport animals of the infantry, some cattle, and the war correspondents; all of which travelled up the west bank of the river. Attached to the 21st from the 4th Hussars, was the young Winston Churchill. Eager to see some action, he had talked Sir Evelyn Wood into arranging a posting. The column arrived safely at Wad Hamed, the advanced base for the expedition. Sixty miles ahead lay Khartoum, now in ruins, and the sacred city of Omdurman, which faces it across the river. Here lay the tomb of the Mahdi, who had died of typhus soon after the death of Gordon.

The Mahdi's successor, Khalifa Abdullah, had at his disposal an army of 60,000 fighting men, guarding Omdurman, while the Expeditionary Force, commanded by the Sirdar, General Sir Herbert Kitchener, consisted of two British and four Egyptian infantry brigades, four squadrons of 21st Lancers, eight companies of camel corps, and nine squadrons of Egyptian cavalry, supported by 44 field guns, 20 Maxims, and ten gunboats – a total of 8,000 British troops and 17,000 Egyptian.

The cavalry led off at dawn on August 27, covering the main body of the force, which moved across country on a broad front, with the river on the left of the marching columns. The first two nights were spent on the river bank at Royan and Wadi el Abid, some six miles apart; on the 29th the force came within sight of a high hill on the river bank – the Djebel Merreh. The 21st Lancer squadrons were concentrated, and sent forward to occupy this vantage point. The hill held no enemy, so one squadron was left in observation; before long a helio signal reported a Dervish mounted patrol moving westwards in front of the cavalry advance guard. The patrol approached the right troop of the 21st, who fired a few shots and drove them away.

This great mass of troops moving across country recalls a little the army moving towards Alma some forty years earlier, except for the fact that no longer did the columns glitter with gold and silver, scarlet and blue; for now the whole army was dressed in khaki. Each evening the troops built a thorn *zariba* round the whole camp site, within which the animals were picketed. The camp on August 31 was within sight of the Kerreri Hills, beyond which lay Omdurman. On September 1, the 21st Lancers, in the advance guard, crested the hills and saw the tomb of the Mahdi in the distance. No enemy were to be seen at first, and the cavalry advanced steadily across an open sandy plain from the centre of which rose the black rocks of Djebel Surgham, three miles from the outskirts of Omdurman, and one mile from the river. All at once, some miles away on the slopes to the right of Omdurman appeared, in Churchill's words, 'a long black line with white spots...it seemed to us...that there might be 3,000 men behind a high dense *zariba* of thorn bushes.' As they watched, this line began to move forward, proving to be not bushes, but the front rank of an enormous mass of men, four miles long, which flowed rapidly over the face of the hill towards the cavalry, who stood 'spell-bound'. At this time, the river gunboats began a bombardment of the defences of Omdurman, while on the far bank, the Arab irregulars attacked the forts on the other side of the river. A howitzer battery, firing very large shells, was landed, and began to bombard the Mahdi's tomb, the dome of which soon disappeared.

By 1 p.m. the Khalifa's huge army had advanced within two miles of the Djebel Surgham, watched by the cavalry and camel corps, who withdrew slowly in front of the moving mass. The rest of the British and Egyptian infantry had now debouched from the Kerreri Hills, and had taken up a position with their backs to the river, half-way between the hills and the Djebel. The regiments stood in a long arc, behind a *zariba*, two deep, with each flank on the river, enclosing the transport, which was gathered among the mud huts of a small village. The two main forces were thus about five miles apart, though not yet in sight of each other. The British infantry ate their dinners – essential prelude to a battle, if time allows. However, the Dervish army halted, fired off their rifles, and lay down on the ground. For the rest of the day, the 21st patrolled and skirmished with the enemy cavalry, returning through the *zariba* at nightfall. The approaches to the camp were swept at night by searchlight from the gunboats. The situation was a dangerous one – a night attack might have overwhelmed the whole expeditionary force; but the enemy were afraid of the lights, and made no move.

At dawn next morning the army 'stood-to' while the cavalry went out on patrol – the 21st on the left towards Djebel Surgham, while Broadwood's Egyptians re-entered the Kerreri Hills. Between the two features the cavalry found the Dervish forces advancing in five masses, each distinguished by the flag of its leader. Away to the right, 5,000 men under the bright green flag of Ali Wad Helu; next, against the Kerreri Hills, 15,000 men led by the dark green of Osman-Sheikh-ud-Din; in the centre, advancing directly on the camp 8,000 men under Osman Asrak; on the western slope of Djebel Surgham, the black flag of the Khalifa himself floated over another 17,000, while between the Djebel and the river lay a square of 6,000 more warriors, topped by many white flags.

The first shots were fired from two small guns in the centre of the Dervish line; the British and Egyptian artillery replied at once, at a range of about 3,000 yards. The 'white flags' on the left of the front came within range of the gunboats and the artillery in the *zariba*, which opened fire with devastating effect. As the cavalry patrols rapidly withdrew from the narrowing space between the two forces, the infantry opened fire. Churchill considered that the Khalifa had completely miscalculated the power of modern weapons, in asking his forces to face such punishment.

As the frontal attack died out under the terrific fire from the *zariba*, the Khalifa put into action the second part of his plan, which was to move his left under Osman-Sheik-ud-Din in an outflanking movement to the north, through the Kerreri Hills. This movement was covered, with some difficulty, by Broadwood's Egyptian cavalry, who found their animals outpaced by the bare-footed Dervishes in the difficult going. Lord Kitchener therefore ordered Broadwood's force to withdraw to the *zariba* to join the 21st Lancers, who were now watering their horses and resting. The withdrawal of the Egyptian cavalry and the Camel Corps gave heart to the Dervishes in the hills, and they pressed forward, cutting off the retreat of the Camel Corps, and threatening to drive them into the river. The situation was saved by two of the gunboats, which opened fire at short range with Maxims, quick firers and rifles. Broadwood lured the remainder of the enemy horsemen away in pursuit of his own cavalry, but in the process, lost two of his Horse Artillery guns in a swamp. However, he drew the Dervish cavalry into the field of fire of the two gunboats, which drove off the Dervishes, leaving Broadwood free to return to the *zariba*, collecting his missing guns on the way.

Even with modern radio aids, this little combined operation between ship and shore would have been difficult enough; Colonel Broadwood was clearly a leader whose control of cavalry was

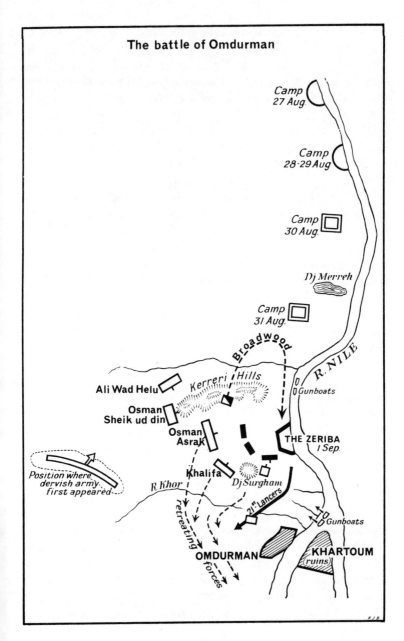

The battle of Omdurman

Camp
27 Aug.

Camp
28-29 Aug.

Camp
30 Aug.

Dj Merreh

Camp
31 Aug.

Broadwood

R. NILE

Ali Wad Helu

Kerreri Hills

Gunboats

Osman
Sheik ud din

Osman
Asrak

THE ZERIBA
I Sep.

Position where
dervish army
first appeared

Khalifa

R. Khor

Dj Surgham

21ˢᵗ Lancers

Gunboats

retreating

OMDURMAN

KHARTOUM
(ruins)

forces

H.J.B.

excellent. Meanwhile, the masses in the centre pressed forward to within 300 yards of the *zariba*, but could get no further. By 8 a.m. the attack was broken – the Dervishes had lost 2,000 men, and the Sirdar's army, perhaps 150. The artillery continued to search out the folds in the plain, flushing parties of the enemy, which were then cut down by the Maxims. Here was the first taste of modern warfare; in Winston Churchill's account, one can detect no satisfaction – only a sympathy for the unfortunate Dervishes who had been driven into this massacre.

Kitchener now felt it essential to occupy Omdurman, before the enemy could withdraw into the city. The 21st Lancers were ordered to stand to their horses; General Gatacre, commanding the British Division, galloped up, and ordered Colonel Martin, the commanding officer, to reconnoitre the approaches to Omdurman. The Regiment moved out in mass, with a few patrols in front; reaching a low ridge, they found the plain between them and the town dotted with small parties of Dervishes, while further away to the west a 'broad stream of fugitives, wounded and deserters' was heading back to Omdurman. A helio signal was sent, indicating the situation, and the reply came back 'Advance and clear the left flank, and use every effort to prevent the enemy re-entering Omdurman'. The regiment, which had halted while the messages were exchanged, now remounted, and two more patrols were sent out, one forward into the plain, and one to the lower slopes of Djebel Surgham. The first patrol soon returned, with the information that 'in a shallow and apparently practical *khor* (stream-bed) about three-quarters of a mile to the south-west...between the regiment and the fugitives, there was drawn up a formed body of Dervishes about 1,000 strong'. (Churchill.) On this information, Colonel Martin decided to attack.

The enemy force reported was in fact a small flank-guard of 700 tribesmen of the Hadendoa, put there by the Khalifa expressly to guard his retreat to Omdurman. Seeing the first movement of the 21st Lancers, the Khalifa sent another four regiments from the Black Flag, to join the Hadendoa, bringing the flank-guard up to nearly 3,000 men. The 21st left their ridge, unaware of this increase in the enemy strength, and rode at a walk, in mass, to within 300 yards of the blue-clad line of Dervishes. Colonel Martin, thinking they were spearmen, decided to move round the left flank, and wheeled across the enemy front at the trot; at this, the Dervishes knelt down and opened fire, scoring several hits; Colonel Martin then ordered his trumpeter to sound 'right wheel into line'; the sixteen troops swung round and charged. Behind the first line of Dervishes suddenly appeared a mass of men, twelve deep, extending almost the length of the cavalry front, hidden in the shallow depths of the *khor*. The two lines, horses and men, met with a crash and a shout, flinging the front line of Dervishes back on to the mass behind. The momentum of the charge carried the squadrons through the enemy and, says Churchill, 'within two minutes every living man was clear of the Dervish mass...all who had fallen were cut at with swords till they stopped quivering....'

The 21st reformed beyond the enemy; out of 400, five officers, 65 men, and 119 horses had been killed or wounded.

This was not the time for Prince Rupert's tactics; the 21st, resisting the inclination to charge again, drew off to the flank, dismounted, and opened fire; the Dervishes, who had also reformed their ranks, changed their front and bravely began to advance; but the fire was too hot for them, and the advance changed to orderly retreat, back towards the Black Flag on Djebel Surgham.

The Victoria Cross was awarded to three members of the regiment during this engagement: to Captain Paul Kenna, who first rescued Major Crole-Wyndham, when the latter's horse had been killed under him, and then returned into the mêlée to help de Montmorency;

– to Lieutenant Raymond de Montmorency, who went back to find Lieutenant Grenfell, who was lying surrounded by Dervishes. He found Grenfell dead, recovered the body and put it on his horse, which broke away. Captain Kenna and Corporal Swarbrick helped him back to the regiment. Montmorency was a grandson of General Michel, under whom the 17th had pursued Tantia Topi in India;

– to Private Thomas Byrne, who though badly wounded, went to the rescue of Lieutenant Molyneux, who was wounded, disarmed, and being attacked by Dervishes. Byrne attacked them, and was wounded again, but this action enabled Molyneux to escape. Meanwhile Kitchener had already ordered the army to start its move on Omdurman; five brigades moved off to the south, while the sixth prepared to follow with the transport. The right hand brigade, composed of Sudanese troops, nearest the gap between Djebel Surgham and the Kerreri Hills, became somewhat isolated, while the *zariba* itself was left exposed. The whole force of the Khalifa's reserve poured out from Kerreri and from behind Djebel Surgham, and threatened to overrun the Sudanese brigade; however, the two nearest brigades wheeled to its help, and drove off the enemy with accurate rifle fire. After beating off a last desperate charge by the Dervish cavalry, the Anglo-Egyptian army drove the remains of the Khalifa's force back into the desert, and continued the march towards Omdurman. The 21st moved towards the stream of fugitives heading back to the city; many surrendered, and others fled southward away from the battlefield. The cavalry pursuit was then held up, while the army rested and drank from the river just outside Omdurman. When all was ready again at about 4 p.m., the cavalry were sent to patrol round the outskirts of the town, while the infantry divisions entered and cleared the streets. As dark fell, the Egyptian cavalry were sent in pursuit of the Khalifa, but after blundering about in the dark, and failing to find a steamer which was to bring them supplies for the following day, the chase was abandoned.

Three days after the battle, the 21st started the long journey back to Cairo. When Queen Victoria heard of the victory, and of the conduct of the regiment, she wrote personally to authorize the use of the title 'The Empress of India's' and a return of French-grey facings for the uniform (the regiment had been unwillingly forced to adopt red facings on their arrival in Egypt). Her Majesty later ordered all ranks to wear the Imperial cypher on their shoulder-straps, a distinction believed to be unique.

Chapter Nine

The South African War

THE SOUTH AFRICAN WAR began in October 1899. This is no place in which to try to describe the origins and causes of the war, which sprang from the discontent of the Dutch-bred Boer element among the settlers in South Africa. The campaign was divided into three phases; in the first, the Boers invaded the British-held territory from the provinces of the Orange Free State and the Transvaal; the British forces were besieged in Mafeking, Ladysmith and Kimberley, all cities near the frontier. Attempts by the British army, under Sir Redvers Buller, to raise these sieges were unsuccessful; the relieving forces suffered one defeat after another at Stormberg, Magersfontein, Spion Kop and Colenso. Buller was replaced in December by Lord Roberts, with Lord Kitchener as his chief-of-staff. Lord Roberts reorganized the army in the field, paying particular attention to the supply and transport services. The British then advanced up the line of the railway towards Kimberley, and concentrated between the Orange and Modder Rivers. From there, Roberts sent General French's Cavalry Division to relieve Kimberley, and with the infantry he himself moved eastwards on Bloemfontein.

French's cavalry division crossed the Modder against the opposition of de Wet, at Klipdrift, and in one of the last great cavalry operations in history broke through the Boers and went on to relieve Kimberley on February 15. A few days later, Cronje's forces surrendered at Paardeburg near Bloemfontein. The pressure in the Orange Free State resulted in an improvement in Natal, where Ladysmith was relieved at the same time. Bloemfontein fell in March, Mafeking was relieved in May, and by June Johannesburg and Pretoria were in British hands. The war seemed to be over; after the annexation of the Transvaal in October, Lord Roberts left South Africa, handing over command to Kitchener; but in fact the real campaign was just beginning.

The second phase started when the Boers, having dispersed their field army, took to guerilla tactics by multiplying the local 'commandos'. They carried out raids on railways, outposts, and convoys; these tough, skilful fighters seemed impossible to catch. The names of the commando leaders became household words in Britain; de Wet, de la Rey, Hertzog, Botha, Beyers and Smuts; they ranged from the Atlantic coast to the Indian Ocean, and threw a new light on the science of mobile warfare.

Kitchener, in the third and last phase of the war, solved the problem of the commandos by dividing the whole country into sections by chains of blockhouses linked with barbed wire, in order to limit the movement of the Boer columns. At the same time, the non-combatant population was evacuated into 'concentration camps' − (the first time the term was used) − in order to prevent civilians from giving assistance to the guerillas.

Shortage of medical supplies and staff, combined with primitive sanitation, resulted in outbreaks of typhus and dysentery. Hundreds of Boer women and children died in these camps, which were the cause of a lasting bitterness greater than that generated by the war itself. The blockhouse system was completed by 1902; British drives within the system finally wore down the Boer resistance, and in May delegates of both sides met and signed the peace of Vereeniging.

The 17th sailed from England on February 14 1900, the day that French's Cavalry Division was nearing Kimberley. With the usual bad luck attending voyages of the 17th, one of the two ships carrying the regiment broke a propeller and arrived a fortnight late at Capetown. The regiment entrained, to join the 3rd Brigade of the Cavalry Division at Bloemfontein in April, just as the first phase of the campaign was ending.

The next eighteen months were to be spent in an almost continuous *trek* in pursuit of the Boer commandos. From April until October 1900, de Wet was the quarry — and he was never caught. The Boers proved to be the most difficult opponents that the British Army had ever met. J. L. Smail, in the preface to his *Monuments and Battles of the South African War*[1], says:

> Boer military philosophy was unique: 'The British fight to die, but we Boers fight to live.' Supply problems which cramped British strategy, hardly existed for the Boer; he carried all he needed on his horse: *biltong*, coffee and a blanket for the night....They were the finest mounted infantry in the world, superb horsemen, excellent shots, and masters at the art of camouflage.

It was against this enemy that the British army had to re-learn the art of war. The improved performance of small arms, machine-guns and artillery meant that a small force could cover a greatly increased front with fire. By skilful use of the natural defensive strength of rocky hills and *kopjes*, the defenders could remain safe from the traditional attack by lance and sword. By the employment of pack horses instead of wheeled transport, the Boer columns retained a superb mobility.

The 3rd Cavalry Brigade chased de Wet all round the triangle between Pretoria, Mafeking, and Bloemfontein, and lost him in the end after six months. Near the end of the chase Sergeant Thomas Lawrence of the 17th was on patrol with Private Hayman, when they were attacked by about a dozen Boers. Hayman's horse was shot, and he fell, dislocating his shoulder. Lawrence put Hayman up on his own horse, and using both men's carbines, kept the Boers off, until Hayman was in safety. He then retired for two miles on foot, keeping the Boers at bay until help arrived. For this action

[1] (Pub: Howard Timmins, Capetown, 1966)

Lawrence was awarded the Victoria Cross.

After the pursuit of de Wet, the 17th returned to Kroonstadt, where the Brigade was broken up into smaller columns. Steps were taken to improve the mobility and fighting power of the cavalry. Lances and swords were discarded, and the short ranging carbine was discarded in favour of the infantry rifle and bayonet. The load carried by the horse was lightened by discarding wallets (carrying spare clothes) and by carrying only two blankets, one each for man and horse. The 17th became dragoons once more, in fact if not in name.

The pursuit of de Wet began again, this time on the borders of the Orange Free State and Cape Colony, around the centre of Steynsburg. All through the winter of 1900 and the summer of 1901 the squadrons twisted and turned, clearing farms, rounding-up stock, burning supplies that could not be carried away, escorting the civilian population into the camps, catching and breaking-in the many stray horses wandering in the veldt.

In June, a new commanding officer was posted to the regiment − Lieutenant-Colonel Douglas Haig, a 7th Hussar, who had recently been a member of General French's staff. In the list of officers at that date, two other names stand out − the Hon. H. A. Lawrence, Brevet Lieutenant-Colonel, and B. D. Fisher, Lieutenant, who were both to play an important part in the future of the regiment.

The blockhouse system was now beginning to function; early in September, news came that General Smuts' commando was in the area, heading for Tarkestad, 60 miles to the south-east of Steynsburg. The 17th was sent down by train, and took up a position on the Elands River with squadrons about four miles apart, the leading squadron being in position at a farm at Modderfontein, about ten miles north of Tarkestad. Colonel Deneys Reitz, then fighting in Smuts' column, describes the battle at Modderfontein in his wonderful book on the war.[1] The commando in which he was fighting was on its last legs, short of horses and starving. A

---

[1] (*Commando*, Deneys Reitz. Faber & Faber Ltd., London, 1929).

Dutch farmer reported that there were English cavalry waiting in the valley; Smuts at once ordered a section forward to locate the British, while he himself brought up the rest of the commando. The advance section, in which Reitz was riding, ran into a troop of the 17th, which at first mistook the khaki-clad Boers for British troops from another column. The Boers opened fire, bringing down several of the 17th; the rest withdrew to a low stony ridge further down the road. The Boer section following them, ran into heavy fire from rifles, a machine gun and a mountain gun.

'We were surprised to see a large English camp, less than a stone's throw away, buzzing like a disturbed ant-heap...our little party was stranded on the very edge of an armed encampment, and practically mixed with the English soldiers. Fortunately General Smuts had hurried the commandos on, and in a few minutes they opened fire from a hill in the rear....'

The fire-fight went on at close range among the rocks — 'they were no match for us in short-range work of this kind,' wrote Reitz. The gun crew was killed; the rest of the squadron fought to the finish, though one troop, posted a little further away, was able to escape after firing all their ammunition, using the last few bullets to shoot their horses. Of a total strength of 140, 4 officers and 32 men were killed, 4 officers and 33 men were wounded. Reitz says:

Having started that morning with a grain-bag for chief garment, a foundered horse, an old rifle and two cartridges, I now appeared in a handsome cavalry tunic, riding breeches, with a sporting Lee-Metford, full bandoliers, and a superb mount, the property of Lieutenant Sheridan. General Smuts now ordered us to set the tents and wagons on fire, and to destroy the guns, as well as such supplies as could not be removed. Then leaving the prisoners, mule-drivers and native servants to shift for themselves, we rode off in triumph.

Modderfontein was a defeat, but not a disgrace, for the 17th. At the end of the First World War, Lord Vivian, one of those wounded at Modderfontein, received this gracious letter from General Smuts:

Dear Lord Vivian — It was a pleasure to meet you again, and to talk over events in the Boer War in which we both took part. What hairbreadth escapes, what tugs-of-war! I see you lying on the ground, badly wounded, on that morning when the 17th Lancers were rushed at Eland's River. How gallantly those boys fought against us, many being killed, because they knew not how to surrender. That fight at Eland's River although a defeat, ought surely always to be reckoned among the most precious records of that great regiment. I only regret that in this war the mounted army has had so few opportunities to distinguish itself.

With good wishes, ever yours sincerely,
N. SMUTS.

For the rest of the Boer War, the remaining squadrons of the 17th were engaged in rounding-up operations among the blockhouse system. Yeomanry or mounted infantry were often attached to the squadrons, for the yeomanry were being used overseas for the first time, as part of the great effort to get as many mounted troops into South Africa as possible. Peace came at last, in June 1902. Let J. L. Smail, author of the quotation about the Boers earlier in this chapter, speak the closing words:

The British were at the outbreak of hostilities described by many as not an instrument of war, but an institution; yet Queen Victoria's army was no ornamental army, her troops had fought in India, the Crimea, New Zealand, China, Persia, Africa, but, except for the Russians, the enemy had always been tribesmen crudely armed, who knew nothing of strategy and used only the most elementary of tactics. The British soldiers did not have the individuality and resources such as the Boers possessed, but for indomitable courage, uncomplaining fortitude, and implicit obedience, they were beyond criticism.

Chapter Ten

World War I

THE BOER WAR had given the nation a severe shock. A small army of farmers had held out for three years against Britain's regular and militia forces, and had given them a lesson in nearly every aspect of warfare.

A Royal Commission was immediately appointed 'to inquire into the military preparations for the war in South Africa...' 114 witnesses, from Lord Roberts downwards, including most of the Army Council, and all the commanders in the field, were interrogated for 55 days. Yet it is hard to find among this heart-searching, much effect upon the cavalry. Cavalry policy still remained one of indecision, so that after 1910 the Lancer found himself, like the White Knight, carrying all three weapons; sword in scabbard on the near side, rifle in rifle-bucket on the offside, lance slung or held by the right hand with its butt in a lance-bucket on the stirrup. To dismount, it was necessary to take the rifle out of the rifle-bucket, replacing it with the lance, which was left on the horse. It is hardly bearable to think what would have happened to groups of led horses under heavy fire.

Besides revising its military training, the twentieth-century army began an era of competitive organized games, which has not yet ended. The officers' sports of hunting, racing, polo and pigsticking had long been popular, and indeed were considered a necessary exercise in horsemanship and courage for the mounted officer, in all arms of the service. Games for the recreation of the soldier had been a feature of army life since the Crimean War; but now regimental journals begin to record a spate of competitions in football, hockey, cricket, boxing and athletics. The Army turned to sport like Mr. Jorrocks, as 'the h'image of war without its guilt, and only five and twenty per cent of its danger'.

Above these ingenuous preparations the wings of the German eagle began slowly to darken the sky, as the world was inexorably drawn into the Great War. Three inventions, the machine-gun, barbed wire, and the internal combustion engine, were about to end the long reign of the horse on the battlefield.

The 17th, on returning from the Boer War, spent three years in Scotland, and then went back to India for nine years. The 21st, having returned from the Sudan in 1899, became bottom of the roll for foreign service, and therefore missed the Boer War; and being sent to India in 1912, was kept there throughout the Great War.

In August 1915, two squadrons and regimental headquarters of the 21st were employed against a force of Mohmand tribesmen who, encouraged by German and Turkish arms and money, invaded the Punjab through the Khyber Pass. On September 5, a battle developed, during which the squadrons charged a body of tribesmen on the far side of an irrigation canal. In the course of the action, Private (Shoeing Smith) Hull won the Victoria Cross for rescuing the Adjutant, Captain Learoyd, whose horse had been shot under him. The Distinguished Conduct Medal was awarded to three Other Ranks in the same action, all for rescuing comrades under fire.

In 1916, the commanding officer persuaded Lord Kitchener to authorize the formation of a Service Squadron to fight in France. The squadron was raised in Tidworth, mostly from reservists, and served in France till August 1917, as part of 14th Corps Cavalry, on the Somme and elsewhere. The squadron was eventually disbanded when infantry losses became so great as to require every possible man to serve in that arm.

The outbreak of war in August 1914 found the 17th at Sialkot.

After some initial anxiety, that the regiment might be stranded in India, horses and men were embarked at Karachi in October, and were transported to Marseilles, as part of the Indian Cavalry Corps, which concentrated at Orleans in mid-November. By this time the mobile warfare, which comprised the opening moves of the campaign, had come to an end. The cavalry had played an important part in delaying the German forces in the retreat from Mons.

However, the 17th took no part in these affairs; by November the German advance had been stopped, and a continuous line of trenches and barbed wire stretched from the English Channel to the Swiss frontier. The cavalry role of working round the enemy flank during the battle was no longer possible – there was no flank. The 17th spent the next three years within an area forty miles wide, round Amiens, taking their turn in the trenches, digging new defence lines, building railways, stopping gaps if the enemy looked like getting through, and training for the day when they might break through, and start in pursuit beyond the trench system. One troop of the regiment acted as permanent escort to Sir Douglas Haig, who was then commanding 1st Corps. Haig, the regiment's fourth Field-Marshal – (Sir Evelyn Wood was the third) – always considered himself a 17th Lancer, although his service with the regiment had been confined to two years in command during the Boer War. He was soon given command of First Army, and in 1915 was appointed Commander-in-Chief of the British armies in France – a post which he held till the end of the war. His policy of attrition, by attacking limited objectives under an enormous weight of supporting artillery, has made him the target for critics; but it won the war in the end, although at tremendous cost in lives. The alternatives were either to win the war elsewhere, or to find some way of breaking the defensive deadlock. The first was outside Haig's province – he was Commander-in-Chief in France, and not Chief of the Imperial General Staff. The critics of the tactics of the Western Front have never succeeded in suggesting any other valid solution. The Allied ventures in other theatres were not successful; the Dardanelles expedition, the Italian front, the campaigns in

Salonika and Mesopotamia were all failures or stalemates; only in Palestine did Allenby's cavalry – Yeomanry and Dominion troops – achieve victory against the Turks. As to the second alternative, on the Western front the search to find a means of crossing wire and trenches under fire was pressed continuously. The idea of the tank was as old as war, but its development, like that of the aeroplane, was delayed until the internal combustion engine became efficient enough to achieve the necessary power-weight ratio. By August 1916, the first detachments of Mark 1 tanks were being shipped out to France, to be tried in action, in the battle of the Somme. The 'males' carried two six-pounder guns and four machine-guns, the 'females' six machine guns. Haig was not slow to see the value of the tank, in fact he was rather too keen to see them in action as soon as possible in support of the infantry. The first tanks achieved surprise, and some success, but the impossible condition of the ground, mechanical failures, and the difficulties of communicating with the infantry, led to many failures and disappointments.

In November 1917 at Cambrai, the British launched a massed tank attack, which had originally been planned by Colonel J. F. C. Fuller, chief staff officer at Tank Corps headquarters. This operation wrote a new chapter into the history of war, since the tank attack was to be made without previous artillery bombardment. The original plan was for a large local raid by tanks; but it became expanded into a full scale offensive, involving two Army Corps, two cavalry divisions, nearly 400 tanks and 1,000 guns. The plan came very near to success; a salient five miles deep and ten miles wide was punched into the enemy lines, but the problem of breaking out from the salient with the reserves proved too much for the exhausted army. The cavalry divisions were unable to contribute anything in the way of exploitation.

At Cambrai, the 17th Lancers were present, in the 1st Cavalry Division, which was actually launched; but the breaking of a vital bridge under the weight of a tank prevented the move forward of reserves at a critical time. A few days later the Germans counter-attacked, and recaptured two-thirds of the ground lost at the start of the battle.

Early in 1918, all Indian cavalry regiments were removed from France to Palestine, while the British regiments remaining in France were regrouped under the British Cavalry Corps. The 17th joined the 7th Cavalry Brigade commanded by Portal, an officer of the regiment. The collapse of Russia in 1917 released a large number of German divisions from the eastern front; and on March 20 1918 Ludendorff launched a tremendous offensive, designed to end the war. The main thrust came between Arras and St. Quentin. The Germans, using comparatively new tactics of 'infiltration' by exploiting only success, and not persisting against opposition, succeeded under cover of a thick fog, in penetrating beyond the reserve line on a wide front. By the morning of March 22 the Fifth Army was in chaos; the Germans were out into open country; the cavalry were sent in all directions to try to fill gaps, cover withdrawals, hold bridges, and even, according to Micholls, 'to do troop drill between the enemy's line and our own *pour encourager les autres*'. One squadron of the 17th was employed escorting German prisoners out of the battle zone; another was attached to the 24th Infantry Division, and acted as divisional cavalry; a third squadron formed part of a combined dismounted regiment, consisting of 200 men from each unit in the Brigade; this dismounted force acted as corps reserve. All these detachments were in action continuously for the first week of the attack; then the Brigade was eventually concentrated once more, and moved to the protection of Amiens, which was threatened. The 17th Lancers were put in support of the 9th Australian Infantry Brigade at Villers-Bretonneux, where a mounted counter-attack by Micholls' squadron — a 600 yard gallop in open order under fire to recapture lost ground — rescued the Australians at a difficult moment. The German attacks died away on April 4. The regiment had at last had a chance to use its mobility in the role of mounted infantry; the officers and men of the 17th had won six M.C.s, one D.C.M., and six M.M.s during these fifteen days.

The Germans attacked again in April, between Ypres and Bethune, and in May between Soissons and Reims, thus driving three great salients into the allied front. But salients in positional warfare soon become traps, unless they can be rapidly linked up. This the Germans were unable to do; all efforts to pinch out the tongues between the salients failed; and in July the Allies, aided by a rapidly increasing flow of American divisions, went into the counter-offensive, with the cavalry in the role of mobile reserve, hoping once more for a break-through. On July 18 the French attacked the Reims salient; on August 8 the British attacked at Amiens − and won a victory described by Sir Basil Liddell-Hart as 'the most brilliant ever gained by British arms in the World War...it unhinged the mind and morale of the German Supreme Command'.[1] Ludendorff declared that 'August 8 was the black day of the German Army in the history of the war'.

The success of August 8 was due to a plan, initiated (according to Liddell-Hart) by Haig himself, in which a mass of 450 tanks was launched, as at Cambrai, without preliminary artillery bombardment. Secrecy, security, deception and diversion were all employed in the effort to gain surprise. As at Cambrai, the attack petered out, partly from a lack of infantry reserves, and partly because the advance ran into the old Somme battlefield, where a mass of rusty wire and old trenches brought all movement to a halt.

The 3rd Cavalry Division, including the 17th, was accompanied by ninety-six whippet tanks, for the role of exploitation. It got within sight of 'perfect cavalry country, bare of trenches or wire, across which parties of the enemy were hastening, with their faces firmly set towards the Fatherland'. (Micholls.) However, enfilade fire from the enemy machine-guns prevented a break-out, and the cavalry were withdrawn into reserve. The whippet tanks were not used imaginatively, but were kept tied to the cavalry. Nevertheless, on August 8, the tide turned for good against the Germans. For the next three months their resistance gradually crumbled.

The cavalry played no spectacular part in the final stages of the war in the west; but in the east, Allenby, with 12,000 horsemen

[1] *A History of the World War 1914-1918*, Liddell-Hart, pub. Faber, 1930.

of the Yeomanry and Dominion forces, planned, fought, and won the battle of Megiddo, annihilating the Turkish army in Palestine, in one of the great decisive battles of history.

Ironically, the success of Megiddo was probably to harm the cavalry more than any other factor in its history; for memories of Megiddo kept alive the belief that horsed cavalry could play a significant role in modern war, and thus obstructed for twenty years the transition from horse to tank, which should have taken place in 1919.

The 17th's casualties in the whole war amounted to 60 killed and 140 wounded; when compared with 101 killed in the Boer War, the figures show clearly how little the cavalry was involved on the Western Front. Many officers of the regiment served with great distinction; foremost among them, Sir Herbert Lawrence became Chief of the General Staff to Haig; Fisher commanded both an infantry battalion and a brigade in action; by a coincidence, Deneys Reitz was to serve under him twice, in command of battalions, fighting as he once said, not *for*, but *with* the British. Many others transferred to the infantry, the yeomanry, or the Machine-gun Corps, or to the new Tank Corps and to the Royal Flying Corps.

As the war ended, the 1st Cavalry Division entered Germany; the 3rd Division remained for a time in Belgium; then in March 1919 the 17th Lancers moved into Cologne. Demobilization decimated the ranks; only a hundred men were left to look after six hundred horses, so a company of the Rifle Brigade was attached to help. Many of these men, after learning to ride, transferred voluntarily to the 17th. It was not until late in 1919 at Catterick, however, that the regiment was made up to strength again. Then 600 recruits arrived from the disbanded 8th Reserve Cavalry Regiment, a unit formed at the Curragh during the War by the 17th. Fisher, who had recently taken over command, found himself with 1,150 men and 300 horses. The Regiment, 'home from the wars' set about the task of reconstruction. In April 1919, the 17th embarked for Ireland, to assist in the Government's attempt to suppress the Sinn Fein. The unenviable task of 'aid to the civil power' brought casualties and death to the Regiment at various times in the two years in which it was employed. Yet the hard conditions of restraint under provocation, and of active service, tempered the new, raw, regiment, into a worthy guardian of the old regimental tradition.

Chapter Eleven

Mechanization

AS USUAL AFTER A WAR, the Army was again reduced in size. In 1921 four cavalry regiments were disbanded – the 5th, 19th and 20th Hussars, and the 21st Lancers. Officers were given the choice of either joining another regiment, of being given leave on half-pay, or of retiring. Those who went to other regiments had hardly had time to get used to their new homes, when the whole of the cavalry was shaken by further alarms. Four more regiments were threatened with disbandment – the 14th and 15th Hussars; the 16th and 17th Lancers. The loss of so many famous regiments could no longer be borne without protest; the cavalry Colonels stirred themselves in defence of their commands. A number of schemes were devised – none of them very satisfactory – before Sir Charles Harris, the Financial Secretary at the War Office, suggested amalgamation. The idea was acceptable to regiments, which now were to bear a double title – 13th/18th, 14th/20th, 15th/19th Hussars, 16th/5th, 17th/21st Lancers. The composite regiment was treated as a complete unit, but squadrons retained the name of their original regiment; thus, in the new 17th/21st, C Squadron was styled C (21st Lancer) Squadron, and wore the 21st Lancer badge. This practice continued until 1929, when Colonels of regiments were called on to decide upon a single badge for their regiments. It was unthinkable to discard Hale's famous motto; compromises were tried, but without success, so the 17th/21st skull and cross-bones.

The new Regiment was quartered at Tidworth, as part of the 2nd Cavalry Brigade. The soldier – now in 1923 to be known as a 'trooper' – still carried lance, sword and rifle; the only sign of modernity was the presence in the Headquarters Squadron of a Machine-gun Troop, of four Vickers guns.

In the 1920s the new Regiment trained and played under Fisher's command with unparalleled intensity. The regimental team dominated Army polo, and even defeated the Argentine team in the Coronation Cup at Hurlingham; a regimental trick ride, trained by Rawlinson, and later by Captain Hurrell, was the sensation of the Royal Tournament at Olympia; the new 17th/21st was, in every sphere, a 'crack' regiment. It was sad that so much of this vitality and skill, not only in the 17th/21st, but in the cavalry as a whole, was devoted to sport, and to training with obsolete weapons.

In the cavalry regimental officers waited for mechanization to come, knowing that it was inevitable. In 1926 a committee had recommended that the cavalry should be mechanized by stages; first the transport, second, the machine-guns, and finally partial replacement of the mounted men by 'cross-country armoured cars'. Yet this committee also recommended the retention of the sword by Hussars and Dragoons, and that *endeavour should be made to obtain an effective weapon of the hog-spear type for Lancers*'! However in 1927, the lance was finally abolished as a weapon of war. It was retained for ceremonial until mechanization; today most regiments own a private supply, and the lance can still be seen on special occasions on dismounted parades. Mechanization went along slowly enough; in 1928 and 1929 the 11th Hussars and 12th Lancers were converted into armoured car regiments; in 1935 and 1936 trials were made with 'motor cavalry' squadrons; in 1937 the 1st King's Dragoon Guards were converted to light tanks; in 1938 the whole of the cavalry followed suit, except for the Royal Scots Greys and the Royal Dragoons.

The news of mechanization came to Lieutenant-Colonel P. V. Harris, commanding the 17th/21st, at the end of the training season in December 1937. The Regiment was then at Meerut, in India, on a tour of foreign service which had begun in 1930. Harris made the announcement himself to the officers, to the sergeants, and in the men's dining halls. He had been told that the conversion should be completed in two years, but on his own initiative he announced that the Regiment would go to camp the following December, fully mechanized. As he left one mess-room, a loud voice behind him said 'the Old Man's gone mad!'

In the New Year of 1938 the Regiment paraded for the last time with horses, which were dispersed immediately afterwards. The process of mechanization was effected by sending a cadre of officers, warrant officers, and N.C.O.s on courses to the Royal Tank Corps schools, and by the attachment to the Regiment of a Royal Tank Corps cadre of one officer (Lieutenant H. E. Pyman), four sergeants and eight other ranks. In order to set a good example, the second-in-command and the Sergeant-Major Riding Instructor, two of the best horsemen in the Regiment, were sent on the first course; both passed with distinction. Thus, from the very beginning, there was no question in the 17th/21st of the 'horsey' character being unsuitable for mechanization. The first motor vehicle to arrive, a Ford car, was pushed from the station by Indian *syces*, with the Regimental Quarter Master Sergeant, not yet mechanized, sitting proudly at the wheel.

By September everyone was trained in tank and wheeled vehicle driving; in October troop training was begun; on December 14, almost a year to the day after the first announcement, the Regiment marched past the Commander-in-Chief in the centre of Delhi, on the way to Brigade Camp.

Training facilities were not very good, the Regiment did no field firing – in fact most of the tanks had no guns. Tactical training in India was extremely limited. The Royal Tank Regiment instructors were of little assistance in this sphere, since their work in India was largely confined to escorting convoys on the North-West frontier. The Regiment devised its own tactical roles, adapting the old cavalry tasks of reconnaissance, protection, and the rapid occupation and holding of ground. Control was rudimentary, since wireless sets were only available down to squadron headquarters;

below that level communication was by flag-signal. Within the tank itself, control was even more primitive — electrical 'intercom' systems not yet being issued, the commander moved off by kicking the driver in the back, steered by prodding his shoulders, and halted by pulling his hair!

It may be worth considering at this moment, how far life in the cavalry helped to make a regiment fit to fight in a mechanized war. First, the climate of the cavalry had always been that of a *corps d'élite*, ever since the days when a man joined, and brought his own horse with him. In peace time the cavalry tended to be filled by officers of independent means, often — though not inevitably — the concomitant of an independent mind. The feeling that a man does not rely on his job for his living, gives him a strength to stand up for his own opinions, but also carries with it the danger that he may not trouble to learn his job properly. Whether this danger is or is not avoided, depends upon the prevailing attitude within a regiment.

In the thirties, promotion was fast in the cavalry, because officers of independent means often retired early. In the 17th/21st one of the subalterns, R. A. Hull, became a captain in four years, whereas in many infantry regiments there were subalterns with up to ten or even sixteen years' service, so great was the post-war blockage in promotion.

In cavalry training, quick deployment in action, with no wasted time, was second nature in all operations. The drills of issuing orders and getting on the move were habitually executed far faster in the cavalry than in the infantry. Junior leaders were taught to strike quickly at the enemy, and to outflank him fast and wide. Accurate and rapid map-reading was essential, and the need for a continuous flow of accurate information about the enemy was paramount in all reconnaissance roles. Administration in the cavalry was, paradoxically, rather too good; there was not enough emphasis upon travelling fast, far and light; the lessons of the Boer War had been forgotten. Horses were inclined to be fattened for inspection rather than fittened for stamina. Although a regiment should have had no administrative tail, on manoeuvres it was too often accompanied by a clandestine column of officers' cars – or Indian servants on bicycles, undoing all efforts of the directing staff to create wartime conditions. Yet horsed soldiering was no sinecure; riding demands skill, courage and physical fitness; stable management requires grinding hard work, and a dedicated care of the animals under one's charge. The men of a well-trained cavalry regiment were splendid material for mechanization, accustomed as they were to quick thinking, rapid movement, and independent action. The men of the 17th/21st soon showed that they could master the tank as well as they had mastered their horses; the pity was that they had not been set to the task ten years earlier.

Chapter Twelve

World War II – Blade Force

THE THREAT OF WAR had acted as a spur during the mechanization of the Regiment; at last, after twenty-five years, soldiering had a purpose. In May 1939, the 17th/21st said goodbye to India's polo and pigsticking for the last time, and sailed for England. At the outbreak of war on September 3, the Regiment was at Colchester, unarmed except for rifles and revolvers, without transport, and brought up to strength by the return, from the reserve, of officers and men without mechanical training. Once again the Regiment was to miss the opening moves of a new war; not until November 1942 was the 17th/21st to sail for battle in North Africa. The three years intervening were spent in the process of forming a complete new armoured division, which in its prime was probably one of the best trained formations ever to leave England. In the meantime, the Regiment, equipped with four old medium tanks, and Vickers machine-guns carried in Austin 'pick-up' trucks, moved around the south and east of England as a mobile reserve against possible enemy landings by sea or by air. After the invasion scare had died down at the end of September 1940, the 17th/21st moved to Marlborough to join the new 6th Armoured Division, which was forming under Major-General J. T. Crocker. The Regiment trained and fought in this formation till the end of the war, brigaded with the 16th/5th Lancers and the 2nd Lothians and Border Horse, in 26th Armoured Brigade.

By 1942 the standard armoured division, after various modifications, was composed thus:

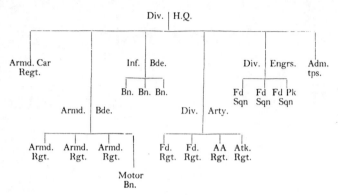

The formation was thus evenly balanced — in the armoured brigade one company of the motor battalion was available to work in support of each armoured regiment; the artillery and the engineers could be divided in support of the armoured and infantry brigades.

26th Armoured Brigade was equipped with Valentine and Matilda tanks, which started to arrive in a steady flow in September 1940. Both were originally designed as 'infantry' tanks, primarily for the support of infantry, as opposed to the lighter and faster 'cruiser' tanks, which were intended for the cavalry role. No British tank at this time was equipped with anything larger than a two-pounder anti-tank gun. The Matilda, soon to become obsolete, was heavily armoured, and was the only British tank capable of keeping out anti-tank fire of any weight.

The winter of 1940 and early 1941 was spent largely in individual training in Wiltshire and Bedfordshire, until April, when the division moved to the area of Newmarket. A whole year was spent in this excellent training area; squadrons went out to camp time and time again, working with companies of the motor battalion, practising control, manoeuvre, and evolving tactical doctrine. By this time, a satisfactory tank wireless was coming into use, containing two sets, one for operating on the squadron frequency,

One of the earliest tanks makes its way through cavalry and infantry in the rear areas in 1916.

Imperial War Museum

The 17th/21st drawn up in review in 6th Armoured Division, waiting for inspection by H.M. King George VI, summer 1941. The tanks are mostly Valentines.

Imperial War Museum

Colonel Hull, Commander of 'Blade Force' receives the DSO from Sir Kenneth Anderson, commander First Army. Sir Richard Hull later commanded both brigade and division in action and was finally promoted to Field-Marshal and Chief of the Defence Staff.

Imperial War Museum

The scene at Thala, on the morning after the night battle, in which the Regiment, harboured in this hollow, stopped Rommel's column of tanks which had broken through the Kasserine Pass.

Imperial War Museum

The fortress of Cassino, seen from Monte Trocchio. The Castle and, above it, the Monastery, look down on the swampy valley of the Gari; away on the left runs the Liri valley, in which the Regiment fought to penetrate the German positions.

Imperial War Museum

In the Appennines, in the winter of 1944, tank crews were forced to live on the road for weeks at a time, barely out of sight of enemy artillery observers on the heights. The tanks are Shermans.

Imperial War Museum

The Regiment on parade formed up as the Motto.

Always prepared to help out the infantry. Lisburn Patrol:
Lance-Corporal Kerry, Trooper Perry, Trooper Welbourne

and one for communication within the troop, or to infantry accompanying the tanks. Early tactical training was devoted to such problems as to whether the troop leader should control his troop by leading it, or by commanding it from behind; how to keep all-round observation on the move; how to apply the doctrine of 'fire and movement'; leaguering at night; camouflage from the air, and so on. It was in an exercise with an Army Co-operation Squadron, that the Commanding Officer, H. C. Walford, was killed, when the aeroplane in which he was being flown, hit a tree and crashed. He was succeeded by Hull, who had already made a name for himself in the Staff Duties branch of the War Office.

Most regimental officers will agree that the squadron or company camp is quite the most pleasant form of soldiering. The squadron commander is master in his own house; the young officers are freed from the tyranny of orderly officer duties; the soldiers from the burdens of ceremonial, fatigues and guard duties. If the weather is good, a squadron camp provides both purpose and relaxation. In the camps on Lakenheath, squadrons were paired with companies from the Motor Battalion, the 10th Rifle Brigade.

General Crocker was an outstanding trainer; his visits to the camps were (in contrast to those of some senior officers) always welcome; he had a happy knack of combining praise and constructive criticism, which commanded great respect among officers and men alike. Mechanization also brought about social changes in the regiment; the officer and his tank crew lived, fed and worked alike, and saw each other continually at the closest quarters. Any deficiency of knowledge, any hesitant decision, was instantly apparent; an officer could not hope to command the respect which is the best foundation of discipline, unless he knew his job backwards, made up his mind quickly, and gave his orders clearly. The functions of the troop sergeant had also changed; in the horsed cavalry he had been undisputed master in the stables, but in the field his duties were confined to taking charge of the led horses. Now he was a tank commander, and more often than not, in war, became a troop leader. The Squadron Sergeant-Major did not ride in a tank, but was responsible for the A Echelon, of petrol and ammunition lorries accompanying and replenishing the tanks in battle. He was therefore removed to a duty which, though supremely important, was rather less glamorous than that of the tank crews. However, in battle, the task of the A Echelon proved to be very difficult and dangerous. The Squadron Quarter-Master Sergeant was in charge of the B Echelon, which formed a mobile administrative base holding reserves of reinforcements, clothing and other necessaries, just outside the immediate battle zone.

In most cavalry regiments, each squadron worked on its own wireless frequency, communicating with regimental headquarters by a single rear-link set. In the Royal Tank Regiment it was the custom to work all tanks of the regiment on one frequency. Each system has its advantages and disadvantages, and the protagonists of both declared that their method was incomparably the best.

In April 1942, the 17th/21st moved to Ayrshire, spending the summer in combined operations training, field firing, and divisional camps, where small forces of all arms were assembled. In August a huge exercise, 'Dry-shod' representing the crossing of the Channel, was followed by a complete re-equipment with new tanks. Each squadron now consisted of three troops of Diesel-engined Valentines, one troop of Crusaders armed with six-pounder anti-tank guns, and squadron headquarters of four tanks, two of which were Crusaders armed with a three-inch close-support howitzer. This useful little weapon fired smoke or high-explosive shell to a range of 3,000 yards, enabling the squadron commander to put down a rapid smoke screen if his tanks ran into trouble. However, the Crusaders were so unreliable and vulnerable, that the squadron leader was often deprived of his weapon at the critical moment.

Re-equipment was soon followed by embarkation orders. Vehicles were waterproofed, stowed with all equipment and loaded at various ports. On November 1 the last parties left for Glasgow by road and train, and embarked, their destination still unknown. What was known, however, was that the 17th/21st was to form the nucleus of a regimental group, commanded by Hull − now a full Colonel. The other members of the group, which was called 'Blade

Force' were an armoured car squadron of the Derbyshire Yeomanry, a battery of twenty-five pounders from 12th R.H.A., one troop of Bofors guns, one six-pounder anti-tank battery, one troop of Royal Engineers, one motor company of the 10th Rifle Brigade, medical and other services, and a tank transporter company. On board ship the plan was disclosed. The convoy contained the 1st Parachute Brigade and most of 78th Infantry Division. The object was to land at Algiers, and to secure French Morocco and Algeria with a view to occupying Tunisia as soon as possible. The parachutists were to drop ahead to capture an airfield, the 78th Division was to advance eastwards from Algiers on the coast road, with Blade Force moving parallel as an inland flank guard, brushing aside any French opposition. However, by November 10, the French had stopped fighting, and when the convoy arrived on November 13, the orders were to move east as soon as possible. It took thirty-six hours to disembark the tanks; on November 15 one squadron left by rail, followed by the remainder of the regiment on transporters. The regiment concentrated at Souk el Arba, guarding the aerodrome captured by the parachutists, after covering 300 miles in a week of bad weather. The leading troops of 78th Division were by now in contact with the Germans at Djebel Abiod, while the Derbyshire Yeomanry had met German armoured cars on the bridge at Medjez el Bab. On November 24, the thrust for Tunis and Bizerta was begun by 78th Division, on a two brigade front − one along the west bank of the Medjerda through Tebourba and Djedeida, supported by elements of 1st U.S. Armoured Division, the other through Mateur to Bizerta. Covering the wide gap between the two, Blade Force was to operate in the area of Sidi Nsir, ready to exploit towards either Mateur or Djedeida.

The Germans reacted very quickly to the Allied landings. By the end of November they had 15,000 fighting troops, 100 tanks, 60 field guns and 30 anti-tank guns in the theatre. But their main advantage lay in the air; the Allies had only the poor grass airfield at Souk el Arba (useless in wet weather), two more at Souk Ahras, and then nothing else nearer than 150 miles from the front. The

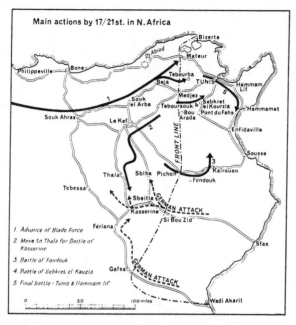

Main actions by 17/21st. in N. Africa

1. Advance of Blade Force
2. Move to Thala for Battle of Kasserine
3. Battle of Fondouk
4. Battle of Sebkret el Kauzia
5. Final battle - Tunis & Hammam lif

Germans had seven concreted airfields near Tunis, and twenty more landing grounds, all within fifty miles.

Blade Force went into action on November 24, capturing three farms south of Mateur, held by Italian troops. Next day, a German armoured counter-attack was held with difficulty by the light tanks of the American armoured regiment; the 17th/21st joined in the battle and helped to recapture the ground lost. The German tanks proved to be armed with the formidable long 75mm gun – effective up to at least 2,500 yards against the Valentines and Crusaders, whose two-pounders were useless over 500 yards. Interest now shifted to Tebourba, where the right-hand brigade of 78th Division was making progress. An American light tank company had raided Djedeida aerodrome, catching forty Stuka divebombers on the ground. Before the infantry could exploit further to capture the bridge at Djedeida, the Germans struck southwards with tanks from the Chouigui Pass, at Djedeida, Tebourba and Medjez. After

88

three days of fierce fighting, the Allies were driven back to the outskirts of Medjez, with all hopes of a rapid capture of Tunis brought to an end. After some skirmishing in the area south of Mateur, Blade Force was withdrawn and disbanded. The Allies had failed to capture Tunis for three reasons: first the disparity of the lines of communication — the Allies' over 300 miles from Algiers, the Germans' never more than 50 miles from Tunis or Bizerte; secondly the overwhelming strength of the German air force, which dominated the battlefield, and denied all movement of unarmoured vehicles by day; thirdly the outgunning of the Allied tanks, with their 37mm and two-pounder peashooters matched against the long 75mm, and the 88mm anti-tank gun.

The actions of the 17th/21st in Blade Force, mostly too small to be detailed here, were very similar to the old style cavalry preliminaries to any war, before the two main forces meet. Now a continuous defence line began to form across the whole front, and the campaign entered into its second stage.

Chapter Thirteen

Victory in North Africa

IN SPITE OF THE SETBACK at Tebourba, and of heavy German pressure at Medjez, the Allied high command still hoped to capture Tunis by Christmas. But terrible weather, and obstinate defence and counter-attack by the Germans at Longstop Hill kept the door to the plains closed. The projected attack on Tunis was finally abandoned; the British First Army in the north was to be husbanded and reorganized, and the armour was to be re-equipped with American Sherman tanks.

The Germans now began to take the initiative. In a series of attacks further south they captured all the passes in the Eastern Dorsale, the long mountainous spine which guards the entry to the coastal plains of southern Tunisia.

Early in January, 6th Armoured Division was at Bou Arada, where the Regiment was involved in several attempts to capture the feature known as 'Two-Tree Hill' a rocky tangle of hills lying west of the lake of Sebkhret el Kourzia. This was the first experience of attacking a fixed position, and it proved too well the ability of the Germans to dig, fortify and hold a defensive position in depth. The position was scarcely dented; the Irish Brigade suffered such heavy casualties that they were withdrawn and replaced by the 1st Guards Brigade, which remained with 6th Armoured Division till the end of the war. A few days later, the Germans attacked Bou Arada with two columns of tanks across bare ploughed fields, and in their turn paid the penalty for neglecting their own doctrines. Attacks followed in quick succession, against the Parachute Brigade at Djebel Mansour, against the French at Robaa, where one squadron of the Regiment was in support; against the Americans at Ousseltia, where a brigade group of 1st U.S. Armoured Division held firm. The formidable Tiger tank with its 88mm gun appeared in Africa for the first time at Robaa.

The Allies were now on the defensive all along the front. The armoured brigade was withdrawn to re-equip, sending sixty drivers to Oran to collect new tanks. At this moment a new threat appeared in the south: Rommel, in command of the southern front, attacked and routed the Americans at Faid Pass on February 14, with 10th and 21st Panzer Divisions, while a third composite German and Italian armoured force, called the Afrika Korps Group, captured El Guettar and Gafsa. The two Panzer Divisions then brilliantly outflanked and destroyed the American forces at Sidi Bou Zid behind the Faid Pass. 10th Panzer Division swung northwards towards Pichon, 21st Panzer Division towards Sbiba, and the Afrika Korps Group headed for Feriana and the Kasserine Pass. The Americans, exposed for the first time to Blitzkrieg, were thrown into complete chaos. The whole southern front was crumbling; allied airfields at Tebessa, and administrative centres at Tebessa, Le Kef, and even Souk Ahras were in danger. It was now a question of rushing every possible reserve down to the area, to plug the gaps.

The 16th/5th Lancers and the 1st Guards Brigade were sent to Sbiba, while the rest of 26th Armoured Brigade was despatched on transporters to Thala, together with 10th Rifle Brigade, the 2nd/5th Leicesters (fresh from England), three field batteries from various regiments, a few anti-tank and A.A. guns. The Kasserine Pass was still in American hands on February 19. One company of the Rifle Brigade and a squadron of 2nd Lothians were sent to stiffen them up. In the night the Germans infiltrated through on to the American positions, and by next morning, the Lothians and Green jackets were alone. This little force, covering the exit to the pass, fought all day, until their tanks were destroyed. Behind them that night the 17th/21st, with the rest of the Lothians, deployed on a little escarpment, ready to counter-attack the pass; but next morning the Germans came on, overrunning the Rifle Company, and formed up for a set-piece attack. Some miles behind the armour, the Leicesters dug furiously on a ridge covering Thala. The Germans were slow to start their attack – exasperatingly slow both to Rommel and to Brigadier Charles Dunphie commanding 26th Armoured Brigade, who could do nothing but sit and wait, since his artillery was out of range behind the Leicesters' position.

At 3.30 p.m. the German formation, a mass of some 30 tanks, 20 self-propelled guns, and 35 half-tracked carriers, started to advance. 26th Armoured Brigade, hopelessly outgunned in the open country, fought back bravely, withdrawing from ridge to ridge under cover of smoke. The Valentines and Crusaders were picked off one by one – Lieutenant-Colonel Dick Hamilton-Russell, commanding the 17th/21st, had three tanks shot under him; the Regiment was soon reduced to twelve tanks.

At dusk, the force withdrew through the Leicesters position, and prepared to harbour in a little hollow beside the road. As the A Echelon appeared to replenish the tanks, a column of tanks came down the road into the Leicesters position, led by a Valentine; on the outside of its turret sat the crew, smoking. The Leicesters, thinking that stragglers from the battle were coming through, woke up too late to realize that the tanks following were Kw IIIs and IVs.[1] The column opened fire, the first few shots hitting an ammunition lorry, which burst into flames. Captain George Ponsonby, Adjutant of the 17th/21st, leapt back into his tank, and in a few moments knocked out three German tanks. In a tremendous fight, which lasted till midnight, seven enemy tanks were destroyed and the Germans withdrew.

During the night enemy infiltrated into the left of the Leicesters' position, capturing a hill which would overlook the armoured brigade at daylight. Dunphie ordered the remainder of the Lothians – now reduced to two troops – to attack and recapture the hill at

[1] Kw – Kraftwagen, short for Panzer kraftwagen or tank.

dawn. Led by their Commanding Officer, this 'forlorn hope' set out and reached the objective, though some of the tanks ran straight into the enemy tank leaguer. The situation seemed to be hopeless; the morning was spent waiting to make a last stand; but the attack never came. More reinforcements began to arrive, including a regiment of American medium guns which had driven 800 miles non-stop from Casablanca. Next morning, after a night of suspense, the Germans had gone, leaving the road thickly mined.

The battle of Thala was a fine example of the fact that it pays never to give up hope, however desperate the situation. The operation had been the subject of a good deal of argument on the German side. Rommel wanted to attack Tebessa, but the Commando Supremo in Rome insisted on making Le Kef the objective. Rommel felt this would bring the attack within range of allied reinforcements from the north; he was looking all the time for this to happen, and allowed himself to be convinced, by even such 'forlorn hopes' as the Lothians' attack at dawn on Leicester ridge, that the Allies were sufficiently strong in tanks to spare a force for an attack of this sort. The German tank columns were, in Rommel's own judgment, poorly handled, and his commanders failed to grasp the essential difference between fighting in desert and hill country. The dispersal of his forces between Pichon, Sbiba and Kasserine helped to weaken his effort at the critical point. The Valentine which had led the attack (decorated with German markings) had been captured from the 17th/21st at Tebourba; it is interesting that the unsuccessful attack on the 16th/5th at Sbiba was led by a captured Sherman.

After Thala, 26th Armoured Brigade was withdrawn to complete its re-equipment with Shermans. Dunphie, who had controlled the battle so bravely, was attached to the Americans to advise them in retraining, while Brigadier 'Pip' Roberts was brought from the 8th Army to take over the Brigade.

The advent of the Sherman revolutionized armoured tactics. The 75mm dual-purpose field gun with which it was equipped, was equally effective against tanks and anti-tank guns. By engaging likely positions the high explosive shells could strip the camouflage from an 88mm gun and kill the crew, before they could even open fire. Once an anti-tank gun was located, it was finished. The armour-piercing shot was effective against all except the heaviest armour plate. The gun was also capable of being used for indirect fire, without exposing the tank to the enemy at all. The Americans had produced a vehicle immeasurably better than any British tank up to that time; the men of the 17th/21st accepted it with gratitude, it was to be their 'mount' until the end of the war.

The armoured brigade was now fought as a single self-contained formation, made up of three groups of all arms, each based on an armoured regiment, a battery of artillery, a company of the motor battalion, a troop of anti-tank guns, and a detachment of engineers.

One squadron of each armoured regiment was organized as reconnaissance squadron, and was given the task of advancing as far ahead and as fast as possible, to find the enemy on a wide front. The two other squadrons would then attack, moving forward under the support of their own guns, and of the artillery battery, whose observer travelled in his own tank. The anti-tank guns watched the flanks for enemy tanks, while the rifle company held a defensive position until required to mop up behind the armour. The engineer detachment acted as advance party for the divisional engineer resources, which were called in if a big obstacle was met. Close behind the tanks and infantry, came the A Echelon, including ammunition, petrol, fitters, and the medical party.

While 6th Armoured Division was refitting, Von Arnim in the north, encouraged by the near success of Rommel in the south, launched a series of savage attacks at Djebel Abiod, Sidi Nsir, Medjez and Bou Arada. Although much important ground was lost, all the attacks were contained, and by the end of March the Allied army was ready at last to turn to the offensive.

6th Armoured Division was now in 9th Corps, which was commanded by General Crocker. General Alexander, who had assumed command of both First and Eighth Armies, now ordered an attack through the Fondouk Pass, into the coastal plain, to cut off the Axis forces retreating in front of Eighth Army. He ordered the American 34th Infantry Division to seize the pass. This formation, practically untried in battle, failed at the first attempt. Alexander therefore sent 9th Corps, with the orders that the pass was to be breached by April 10 at the latest. The pass is a flat river plain about 1,000 yards wide between two low rocky ridges; on the left the Djebel Rohrab, on the right the Djebel Aouareb. The Axis forces holding the pass, which was heavily mined, consisted of about five battalions of infantry (including one composed entirely of court-martial offenders being rehabilitated) thirteen anti-tank guns, artillery and mortars.

Crocker's plan was to capture the high ground on the left with the British 128th Infantry Brigade, and the ridge on the right with 34th U.S. Infantry Division; then to pass 6th Armoured Division through, with either the armour or the Guards Brigade leading, depending on the circumstances. However, though 128th Brigade was largely successful, 34th Division failed again. Crocker, with his time limit running out, ordered the commander of 6th Armoured Division to try the pass. A preliminary reconnaissance by B Squadron of the 17th/21st, commanded by Major Charles Nix, approached the minefield, and ended in the loss of four tanks to defiladed guns, which in the dust and smoke were impossible to locate. Efforts to breach the minefield in the night with engineers and riflemen were unsuccessful. At dawn, a battalion of Welsh Guards was sent to clear Djebel Rohrab on the left, but by 9 a.m. both sides of the pass were still in enemy hands. Crocker had no alternative left; he sent for Roberts, and ordered him to send the armoured brigade through the gap, regardless of the fact that the minefield was intact, and both flanks were still held by the enemy.

To the 17th/21st fell the lot of leading this modern 'Charge of the Light Brigade.' When Hamilton-Russell had given the orders to the squadron leaders, Nix, who was to lead the attack, said to the others – 'Goodbye – I shall never see you again.' One is reminded of Lord Cardigan saying, 'Well, here goes the last of the Brudenells.'

When the advance began, a torrent of fire fell on the tanks; many were blown up on mines, others were destroyed by anti-tank guns; one troop of the leading squadron got right through, reaching a feature called 'the Pimple' beyond the pass, before all its tanks were destroyed. Micholls, son of the author of the second volume of the Regimental History, was leading this troop, and was never seen again. Nix continued to fight with his tank, and to control the squadron, until he too was killed; B squadron was reduced to a strength of two tanks. The crews of the knocked-out tanks lay on the bare plain under fire from mortars, artillery and snipers. Sergeant Melling, after knocking out an anti-tank gun, and silencing several machine-gun posts, was ordered to withdraw. Instead, he advanced and rescued twenty-three men of the other crews, bringing them back on his tank. He was awarded the Military Medal.

C Squadron advanced behind B, further to the right; but after losing both leading troops on mines, they were withdrawn.

A Squadron, commanded by Ponsonby, the hero of Thala, made more progress by the edge of the dry river, on the left flank. By 11.30 a.m., fire from Djebel Rohrab was silenced by the Welsh Guards, and Roberts ordered the 16th/5th Lancers to try the river-bed. In one and a half hours, they were through, and turning to attack 'The Pimple', on which was found the wreckage of seven anti-tank guns.

A German counter-attack with a few tanks held up the break-out from the pass till dusk; next morning the advance was continued, but the German rearguards had slipped northwards through Kairouan. 26th Armoured Brigade went out in pursuit, but the chase died out at Sbikha two days later.

The German force at Fondouk had done its task − the 'Criminals' had earned their remission. The battle led to some fierce recriminations. Crocker's strictures on the state of training and morale of 34th U.S. Division were countered by accusations that he had ignored American protests about the dangers of flank fire from Djebel Rohrab, and had used American troops to bear the brunt of the fighting. The press in England poured oil on the flames by publishing an account saying that Kairouan was captured by U.S. forces; the press in America had built up hopes of a great American victory; the disappointment was of double intensity. The

American army in Africa, however, took the matter seriously, and embarked on a searching programme of analysis and retraining. Fondouk was to be their last serious debacle; they were now to play an increasingly effective part in this and future campaigns.

While the battle of Fondouk was being fought in the south, the infantry of First Army were fighting desperately in the mountains between Djebel Abiod and Medjez to regain the ground lost to Von Arnim in March. Immediately the battle for Fondouk was over, preparations began for a full-scale offensive to recapture Tunis and Bizerta. There were three possible entrances to the Tunis plain — the Bou Arada Gap, blocked by a strongly held defile at Pont du Fahs; the Goubellat plain, backed by broken country north of the Sebkhret el Kourzia — this was not strongly defended; lastly, the main road Medjez-Tunis — the best tank country, but barred by very strong positions on the Medjerda and at Longstop Hill.

The Army plan was for 5th Corps to break in at Medjez, while 9th Corps (including 6th and 1st Armoured Divisions) was to capture the Two-Tree Hill feature west of Sebkhret el Kourzia, and then to make an armoured thrust north-eastwards towards Massicault, to attract and destroy the enemy armour, and to threaten the rear of the forces opposing 5th Corps.

In 9th Corps, 46th Infantry Division was to capture Two-Tree Hill, then the two armoured divisions were to advance to the area of Djebel Bou Kournine north of the lake, and thence north-eastwards towards Massicault. The two armoured divisions reached the area of Kournine, but this high rocky feature was never taken. From its almost impregnable summit observers directed a merciless artillery fire on the British formations, which were followed about by shelling through all the long hours of daylight. Henschel 'tank-buster' planes armed with heavy cannon were also used with some success. The Germans skilfully deployed a screen of tanks and anti-tank guns, and fought the two British divisions to a standstill after five days' continuous fighting. The 17th/21st were in the thick of it throughout. It was a true tank-versus-tank engagement; the Regiment was reduced at the end of four days to a tank strength of nineteen, after what many thought to have been the most unpleasant battle of the whole campaign. The immediate objective — Djebel Bou Kournine — seemed impossible to capture, and useless if it was taken. The subsidiary intention — to destroy the enemy armour — never filtered down to the troops, who felt the whole affair to have been abortive. However, the battle was in fact decisive, since it not only reduced the enemy tank strength to half and destroyed the best of his anti-tank artillery, but it also drained the last of his petrol reserves. German observers detected the exact instant on April 25 that the British armoured divisions broke off the battle, but the Germans were unable to move their own armour back to the Medjez front in time to prevent the break-through there. 1st Armoured Division was left in the Bou Arada area. 6th Armoured, and 7th Armoured from Eighth Army were moved in great secrecy to the Medjez front, and on May 6 after a break-in by 4th British and 4th Indian infantry divisions, on a 3,000 yard front, the two armoured divisions were launched side by side astride the road to Tunis. It was soon clear that the enemy morale was collapsing. Crack German troops were coming out and driving themselves in to surrender. 7th Armoured Division was directed on Tunis, while 6th Armoured, led beyond Massicault by the 17th/21st, headed for Hammam Lif, the entrance to the Cap Bon Peninsula, now the last refuge of the Germans. Here a narrow gap of 800 yards between the sea and the hills was filled by minefields, and by the houses of the little seaside town. The position was held by a division of top-class German troops, supported by 88mm anti-tank guns, and a few tanks. The Germans expected to hold the gap at Hammam Lif for five days. 6th Armoured Division cracked it in twenty-four hours. On the first afternoon the Welsh Guards, supported by the Lothians, captured the north end of the ridge above the town. Next morning, 700 rounds from the divisional artillery were fired into the town, the guns switching from block to block on the street plan. By midday the Lothians were into the north edge of the town, and the Regiment was ordered to make a dash through the sea. Driving at full speed in the surf, letting off smoke, the tanks got through with the loss of only two. By dark they were five miles on, and harboured in a wood, without infantry support, for the night. Orders came, rather to everyone's dismay, to push on in the dark, and capture a *wadi*crossing four miles on. Advancing in single file on the road in the dark, the Regiment met the fire of four anti-tank guns, and stopped short to wait for dawn. As the tanks moved out of leaguer at 4.30 a.m., the Germans opened fire, but all their shots went high, and the guns were soon destroyed. After refuelling, the advance was continued at full speed for Hammamet. The Regiment was held up four miles short of the objective, by a blown bridge covered by anti-tank guns. 20th Guards Brigade took over, allowing the armour to withdraw and rest. On this day enemy prisoners began to appear in overwhelming numbers; next day, May 12, General Freyburg and General Keightley received the surrender of General Graf von Sponeck, commanding 90th Light Division. The war in Africa was over.

Hammam Lif was perhaps the finest achievement of 6th Armoured Division. General von Broich, commanding the 10th Panzer Division, said afterwards that he considered the break-through of a complete armoured division at this defile to be impossible. However, the tank was never again to dominate the battlefield as it did in Africa. New weapons, new methods, and above all new country lay ahead. For the time being, the Regiment relaxed by the sea, and watched the Germans rolling in to prison camps. After victory parades and a visit from His Majesty, the division withdrew to a camp in the hills at Robertville, between Philippeville and Constantine, in a good tank training area. But tanks and wheeled vehicles were soon removed for use elsewhere; the flow of replacements was slow. While Sicily was invaded and conquered in July, and Italy was invaded in September, the armoured regiments trained, and fought against jaundice, malaria and boredom. When the rains came in November, conditions in the camp became even more uncomfortable, and regimental rivalries sharpened into squabbles. The armoured brigade sat on the same hillside for nine months waiting till the next call should come. At last, in March 1944, the 17th/21st embarked for Italy.

Chapter Fourteen

World War II – Italy

THE REGIMENT, after disembarking at Naples, was concentrated at Piedimonte d'Alife, twenty-five miles behind the front line, which was then at Cassino. Training was at once started, with particular emphasis on support of infantry in the set-piece attack. A series of exercises was carried out with all the battalions of 4th Infantry Division.

The American Fifth Army, after originally closing on the Cassino position, had handed over the eastern end of the line to the Eighth Army, now commanded by Sir Oliver Leese. General Sir Bernard Montgomery had departed for England, taking with him much of the former Eighth Army. Thus the Eighth Army in Italy comprised most of the old First Army under another name.

Preparations were in hand for the final breaking of the Gustav line, the strong German defence system which ran across Italy from Termoli on the Adriatic to Minturno on the Mediterranean. The key to this line lay at Cassino, one of the strongest defensive positions in the world, and one of the few places in the Second World War where the fighting achieved a ferocity equal to tfhat of the First.

Beyond the Gustav line, hinged on to it behind Cassino, lay a second line, known as the Adolf Hitler line; this ran through Aquino, to the sea near Terracina. Both these lines were strongly fortified with concrete and steel. A third line, the Caesar Line, was

The Colonel-in-Chief watches the Band practising First Aid under
he eye of the Bandmaster WO1 Judd.

Challenger at speed in the Gulf War.

Piers Hankinson

Past and present — the Trumpet-Major sounds the charge on the Balaclava Bugle.

A.T.V. Ltd

based on the Alban Hills, but was not completed. Beyond this, the Allies had established a bridgehead at Anzio, which the Germans had succeeded in containing since February. There was then no other fortified German defence line nearer than the Gothic line, two hundred miles to the north; the Gothic line ran through the high mountains north of Florence, from Pesaro to La Spezia.

General Alexander's plan was to trap the Germans south of the Tiber by breaking through the Gustav Line at Cassino, making at the same time a sortie from the Anzio bridgehead to cut off the retreating Germans among the Alban Hills at Valmontone. The task of breaking the Gustav line was given to the Eighth Army. 10th Corps was to secure the right flank in the mountains, the 2nd Polish Corps was to isolate the Cassino monastery, and strike down on to Highway 6, the main road to Rome; 13th Corps was to force a bridgehead over the River Gari below Cassino, join the 2nd Polish Corps and thrust through the Liri Valley towards the Hitler Line.

On the left, the Fifth Army, consisting of four French divisions and the American 2nd Corps, was to put in a parallel attack. In reserve were the 1st Canadian Corps and 6th South African Armoured Division.

6th British Armoured Division was in 13th Corps, and its armoured regiments had the specific task of supporting 4th Infantry Division (with whom they had been training) in the 'break-in' across the Gari. The river was between thirty and sixty feet wide, with steep banks and a swift current over six feet deep. In the valley beyond, in thickly wooded, broken, and marshy terrain, the Germans had put wire, pillboxes, concrete bunkers and tank turrets set in the ground. The whole valley was overlooked from the hills on both flanks, by German artillery observers, who controlled about 230 guns and rocket mortars. At the time of the attack, the positions in the Liri Valley were only held by about four battalions, against which the Allies were to attack with eighteen battalions supported by tanks.

The attack began on May 11, under a barrage from a thousand guns, an hour before midnight. The infantry crossed the river in boats, and with great difficulty, established a bridgehead on the

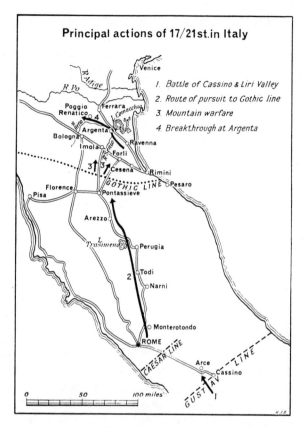

Principal actions of 17/21st.in Italy

1. Battle of Cassino & Liri Valley
2. Route of pursuit to Gothic line
3. Mountain warfare
4. Breakthrough at Argenta

further bank, but no bridge could be built until darkness came on the following evening. In the early hours of the morning, the Regiment moved down to 'Amazon' bridge site, to find all the bulldozers knocked out, and the bridge still incomplete. Lieutenant Wayne, commanding the leading troop, used his tank to help the engineers to push the bridge across the river; the 17th/21st then filed across to join up with the infantry. The tanks were immediately held up by another obstacle, a marshy stream called the Pioppetta. A scissors-bridge tank accompanying the Regiment was knocked out by fire, so Lieutenant David Newbury and his troop of A Squadron, pulling down some trees with tow-ropes, contrived a bridge over which the whole squadron passed. Newbury led on through mines and booby traps, until the tanks reached the Hampshires' position by dusk. Newbury was awarded the M.C. for this enterprising action. By May 14, nine bridges had been built on the Corps front. The next two days were spent in continuous fighting through the thick tangled country, towards Aquino. On May 16, General Vietinghoff gave the order for the Germans to abandon the Gustav line. There was no panic withdrawal — the rearguard fought stubbornly back to the Adolf Hitler line, which was reached by the Allies on May 18. The line was so strong that five more days were needed before it was breached by the Canadians. 6th Armoured Division was reformed and was ordered to prepare for the pursuit. The infantry strength of the division had been increased by the addition of two more motor battalions — thus the division now consisted of an armoured brigade, a motor brigade, and an infantry brigade, with supporting arms as before.

Cassino had been the hardest battle of the war for the 17th/21st — '*this is real war, and makes Africa seem a picnic*', wrote Major Sam Buxton, the Commander of B Squadron. Cassino contained all the elements of warfare in Italy; difficult broken ground seamed with marshes, rivers and gullies, merciless artillery fire directed from mountain observation posts; brave and skilful defensive fighting by the Germans; beauty — here fireflies and nightingales — amid the desecration of war.

With the Hitler line breached, the Germans had only two more delaying positions on the road to Rome; a defile south of Arce guarded by two hills, Monte Grande and Monte Piccolo; and then the Caesar line, incomplete and unmanned. They made a brave stand before Arce, imposing two days' delay on 6th Armoured Division. The 17th/21st were heavily shelled in harbour before the attack on Monte Piccolo, losing Buxton and Wayne who had fought so well at Cassino. The Chaplain Frank Martin, who had been with the Regiment since 1942, was also killed. He had won the hearts of all the Regiment by his unflinching devotion to the work of chaplain in war — a duty which includes not only the spiritual care of the living and dying, but the grim task of identifying and burying

103

the dead, often horribly charred among the wreckage of burnt-out tanks.

The enemy abandoned Monte Grande and Monte Piccolo on the night of May 28, at the same time as the Allied forces in the Anzio bridgehead broke out towards the Alban Hills. However, the trap was not closed at Valmontone, as General Alexander had intended; the pursuing forces of Eighth Army became jammed on the inadequate roads, while General Mark Clark diverted the American formations heading north for Valmontone, and redirected them westwards to Rome. The Germans, improvising desperately, under heavy attack from the air, succeeded in extricating their forces to the safety of the far side of the Tiber, and in bringing four new divisions from the north, so that by the time the Allied armour got free and took up the pursuit in earnest, the Germans were once more balanced for an orthodox rearguard action.

There are only three roads running northwards from Rome capable of sustaining the weight of a mechanized corps; the Via Aurelia which runs up the coast to Pisa; the Via Cassia, through Viterbo and Siena to Florence, and the Via Flaminia which follows the Tiber to Perugia and Arezzo. The American Fifth Army was to advance on the left, the Eighth Army on the right; the 2nd Polish Corps faced the enemy on the east coast. The factors which prevented a break-through in the pursuit were four — first the increasing power of anti-tank weapons; secondly widespread demolitions by the Germans; thirdly the use of mines and booby traps; lastly, the difficulty of the Italian terrain.

In the early days, the German dual purpose A.A.-anti-tank 88mm gun had dominated the British tanks, which were armed only with solid shot; next, the advent of the Sherman 75mm, which could fire H.E. shell had swung the balance in favour of the tank. Now the Germans produced self-propelled anti-tank guns with enormously thick front armour which were extremely hard to knock out; in addition, the new 'personal' anti-tank weapons carried by the German infantry were now appearing in great numbers. These were powerful 'hollow-charge' grenades launched from simple tubes ('panzerfaust' or 'bazooka'), giving the infantryman in close country or in streets the power to destroy tanks at short range.

Italy is a country perfectly adapted for the use of demolitions in the defence. It is seamed with a network of rivers and deeply eroded streams; every mile of road contains bridges, culverts, cliffs, cuttings and embankments, all of which can be destroyed to hinder the pursuer. In this trail of destruction, to advance, even without opposition, was a major engineering problem. Between Cassino and the Gothic line, the engineers of 6th Armoured Division built 50 bridges in 107 days. Each demolition was not only mined and booby-trapped, but covered by artillery fire controlled from the hill-troops, by tanks and anti-tank guns concealed anywhere within 4,000 yards of the obstacle, and by small arms fire from infantry dug-in nearby. Thus the passage of a demolition could be a long process of unlocking the defences; first a bridgehead would have to be captured, then the tanks and anti-tank guns had to be located and destroyed, then the mines and booby traps removed, and the rubble cleared by bulldozers; a bridge site prepared; a bridge brought up and built in darkness. Finally the advance guard would go through, to find another similarly defended obstacle in the way a few miles further on.

In spite of all these difficulties, the Allies might have caught and destroyed the retreating Germans had one other hindrance not been imposed upon General Alexander. At the critical moment of the pursuit, no less than seven divisions − four American and three French − were withdrawn from Italy for the futile Operation 'Anvil' the invasion of southern France which the American high command had insisted upon carrying out.

The loss of these divisions left the Germans with an adequate superiority in numbers, to enable them to carry out a skilful withdrawal to the Gothic line, lasting for four months. The armour was continually in action, day after day. The principal actions of the 17th/21st were fought at Monte Rotondo, Cantalupo, Marsciano, and Perugia. The enemy then made a prolonged stand of ten days at Arezzo, where 6th Armoured Division finally turned the position, reaching the River Arno after heavy fighting. The advance continued slowly northwards down the Arno valley, with the strain beginning to show clearly among all the units of the division. Three months in the line, a steady drain from battle casualties, and battle exhaustion – the 'shell-shock' of the First World War – had taken their toll. There was no opportunity to train reinforcements, no time to rethink tactical doctrines to meet the new conditions. As the Germans withdrew into the mountain stronghold of the Gothic line, in early September, the armoured regiments were withdrawn for their first rest since the battle of Cassino.

The original plan for the assault on the Gothic line, was for 10th and 13th Corps to attack from Florence towards Bologna. Owing to the difficulty of organizing an attack over high mountain passes, where long stretches of road had been demolished, the focal point of the attack was switched to the east coast, where the Polish, Canadian, and 5th British Corps had been concentrated. The attack was made early in September; in spite of heroic efforts by the Allied infantry, in some of the fiercest fighting of the war, the Germans managed to prevent the opening of a gap through which 1st Armoured Division, now commanded by Hull, could be passed. The enemy left flank was gradually pressed back beyond Rimini and Cesena to Ravenna. But the Romagna – the flat plain north of the Apennines, proved a disappointment. Far from being good tank country, it turned out to be seamed with ditches, canals and rivers with high flood-banks; while in the autumn rains the ground became impassable for even tracked vehicles.

While the main weight of the attack was applied on the east coast, 6th Armoured Division helped to put steady pressure on the enemy centre in the mountains. Here, the inescapable tactics of mountain warfare had to be applied. First, seize the heights on either side of the valley, with infantry, who must be supplied by mule trains. Next, tanks and infantry advance in the valley in order to secure a bridgehead around the next demolition; repair the demolition, advance to the next, seize the next lot of heights, and repeat the process indefinitely. The 17th/21st spent the whole winter, with one short break, in this type of warfare. First in their tanks, trying always to get even one tank on to the high ground to support the infantry; trying to get surprise by finding an unexpected detour, or by laying a scissors bridge; trying to rush the next bridge before the enemy could demolish it. Later, as the infantry grew tired, the cavalrymen left their tanks, and took their place in the line, manning machine guns, and mortars, patrolling in the dark, ambushing the enemy, living and fighting as infantry. Sometimes the tanks took over the tasks of the artillery, registering targets by indirect fire, establishing O.P.s, and supporting the infantry in exactly the same way as the gunners. It was a war of improvisation in which no one could say 'that's not my job'. Casualties were light, since there was very little close contact with the enemy; only on one unhappy day, a few shells fell on the small house in which Regimental Headquarters was sited, killing the Signal Officer, the Intelligence Officer and the new Chaplain, and severely wounding Ponsonby, the second-in-command, the duty officer and five other ranks.

The Regiment had a base at Pontassieve near Florence, in a large country house, to which crews out of the line could be withdrawn to rest. In mid-November, the break mentioned above occurred, when the whole regiment was ordered off to Bari in south-eastern Italy on a special mission. The Regiment was to be equipped with armoured cars instead of tanks, and with new lorries and a lavish scale of special equipment for independent operations. The Regiment moved down to Bari by road, picking up the unfamiliar American 'Staghound' armoured cars on the way. On arrival, the Regiment came under the command of H.Q. Land Forces Adriatic – a formation whose administrative standards fell sadly below those of 6th Armoured Division. Bivouacked on a bare rocky plateau, outside the squalid town of Torritto, on a site where the total amenities consisted of one water tap, and one leaky Nissen hut, the men of the 17th/21st learned that they were to invade Zara in Jugoslavia in co-operation with the 2nd Special Service Brigade. After five days intensive training, in which the new vehicles and weapons were rapidly mastered, the whole operation was called off.

Training continued, however, and before long the Regiment was moved to Taranto, with orders to prepare to embark for Greece. At the eleventh hour, this order was also cancelled, and after a riotous Christmas, the Regiment returned to Florence, to resume the tasks of infantry in the mountains.

This interlude shows to what a great standard of technical flexibility the 17/21st was trained. The Regiment was able, at a few hours' notice, to change its role from tanks to infantry or artillery: to move hundreds of miles and re-equip itself in five days with a completely strange vehicle; to do all this in the field in the depths of winter, with the minimum assistance by instructors from outside the Regiment. They had learnt a lesson which seems to elude some armies – *that war is fought by men and not by equipment*, and that the priceless treasure of a team of good men, led by good officers, can and will take on any task that is asked of it. Conversely, the finest weapons in the world, if manned by incompetent and undisciplined troops, are useless.

As the spring approached, the snows melted and the Germans were gradually forced back out of the mountains, until the towers of Imola and Bologna were clearly visible to the troops on the heights. February had been fine, the ground was rapidly drying up, and for once the weather seemed to favour the Allies.

The Combined Chiefs of Staff were not very interested in Italy; for them the war was to be won on the western front; they milked Italy of three more divisions and two fighter groups, and told General Alexander to contain the German forces, prevent their withdrawal, and take advantage of any weaknesses.

That great general, however, had other ideas. 'I considered,' he wrote in his dispatches, 'that I might be able to do something more drastic.' His new plan was to destroy the German armies in Italy, by encircling them between the Eighth Army on the right, and the Fifth Army on the left.

The plan turned upon the geography of the Po Valley. The mountain streams which ran north-eastwards away from the Fifth Army front, became barriers in the plain lying across the Eighth Army's path. In the plain these rivers often ran above the level of the surrounding land, being contained by high flood-banks and levees, which were a formidable obstacle to tanks and infantry alike. When the banks were breached, the rivers overflowed the land, large areas of which were flooded.

By December, the Eighth Army had reached the east bank of the Senio, beyond which lay three more rivers, the Santerno, the Sillaro, and the Idice. These, however, did not flow directly into the sea, but were all gathered into the Reno, which encircles Bologna from the west, and at San Agostino turns south-eastwards to join the Senio some ten miles from its mouth. North of the Reno, therefore, lay a tract of land comparatively free from major water obstacles. The way to this promised land lay through a narrow gap between the marshy landlocked Lake Comacchio, and the Reno itself. South of the Reno lay a great expanse of flooded country, south of which, in turn, was a tract of better going, bounded by Highway 9, the main road from Rimini to Bologna. Beyond Highway 9, lay the foothills of the mountains in which the Regiment had been struggling all winter.

The vital gap contained two key points, Bastia, where the main road crosses the Reno, and Argenta, which guards the exits to the west.

If the Germans withdrew from Italy, they had to go to the north-east, first behind the Po, then to the Venetian line, based on the Adige and Euganean hills. The Argenta gap was the hinge on which the German front must pivot. If this hinge was broken, withdrawal would be impossible, and the German army would be annihilated south of the Po.

The task of breaking the Argenta defences was given to the Eighth Army. There was no disguising the importance of the Argenta gap. Surprise, therefore, was essential; it was obtained by simulating preparations for a landing from the Adriatic, north of the Po; by attacking towards Bologna in the area of Lugo, to persuade the enemy that this was the main thrust; and lastly by the employment of 400 amphibious tank-carriers, known as Fantails, which had been allotted to the Italian theatre, and the existence of which was unknown to the Germans. In these vehicles, the 9th

Armoured Brigade, commanded by Brigadier Ronald Cooke, a 17th/21st Lancer, was to make a waterborne outflanking movement, to get behind the enemy defences in the Argenta gap.

The role of 6th Armoured Division was that of mobile reserve for the Army. It was a return at last to the old cavalry role of break-through, which the Division had executed so brilliantly in Africa, but which had proved so difficult in Italy. The Division was to be prepared either to break out of the Argenta gap, north of the Reno, or to exploit beyond Lugo, should the Army's southern flank achieve more success. D-day was to be April 10; two days later Fifth Army was to strike northwards west of Bologna; the two armies were to meet somewhere near the bend of the Reno at San Agostino.

On March 19, the 17th/21st moved over to the Adriatic coast to the little town of Porto San Giorgio, 130 miles from the front line. Here they trained with 1st Guards Brigade, studying the support of infantry in the new conditions which would be found in the Po plain. The country would be absolutely flat, intersected by watercourses, and covered with orchards of fruit trees coming into leaf. Thus, while an infantryman lying down could see a hundred yards, under the trees, a tank commander, with his head among the branches, could see for only twenty. Many of the farms had tower-silos, giving good observation for the defenders, while the attacker's artillery observers, travelling in tanks, could see nothing. To counter the heavy Tiger and Panther tanks, the armoured brigade was re-equipped with Shermans carrying a heavier gun, the 76 mm, and a proportion of Shermans armed with the British 17-pounder anti-tank gun, a long unwieldy weapon, which projected so far beyond the tank, that it frequently hit the ground crossing a ditch, breaking off the elevating gear. On April 4, the Division started to move towards the front. On the same day, General Sir Richard McCreery, who had succeeded Sir Oliver Leese as commander of Eighth Army, summoned all his commanding officers to Cesena, and outlined the coming battle to them. He stressed the fact that the Army, though now like a careful old steeplechaser, must seize the opportunity to destroy the enemy before he could withdraw further to the Venetian line, or even to a possible Alpine fortress in Austria. Morale in Eighth Army was in an uncertain state at the time; desertions were common; the war was nearly over, and every man knew that if he survived the coming battle, he had probably survived the war. The authorities, through the medium of the Army Education Corps, had seen fit to flood regiments with plans for demobilization, post-war educaton and other matters which were quite as disturbing to morale as enemy propaganda. Yet General McCreery's call for action was obeyed as implicitly throughout the Army as the trumpet call at Balaclava. The author, who had the honour to be commanding the 17th/21st at that moment, explained the Army plan to the whole Regiment behind closed doors in a village school. The feeling that at last there was a chance to strike a death blow, acted like a tonic; a thrill of excitement ran through the listeners.

However, the task of passing a reserve armoured division through a corps in battle, on one road, is calculated to take the edge off any troops. On April 9, when the attack began, the Regiment was still near Rimini fifty miles behind the lines, with crews working on the new tanks, fitting new tracks, camouflage, and extra armour. All moves had to be made by night, since the armoured reserve must be concealed from the enemy air reconnaissance. During the move up, a regimental group was formed with 7th Rifle Brigade, commanded by Lieutenant-Colonel Douglas Darling, D.S.O., M.C. The battle went according to plan; the New Zealanders crossed the Senio; 56th Division made the amphibious 'hook' in Lake Comacchio to outflank the enemy; 78th Division passed through to clear Bastia; 56th followed to clear Argenta; on April 18, 6th Armoured Division was released from Army reserve, and was ordered to break out beyond Argenta, directed on Bondeno. The 17th/21st group, being in divisional reserve, was the last to go into action. After a series of exhausting night marches, on the afternoon of April 19, the Regiment was ordered to pass through the 16th/5th Lancers, and to capture the bridge over a side tributary of the Reno at Segni, seven miles ahead. The Regiment advanced across country, through orchards and farms held by enemy infantry. When darkness fell, squadrons leaguered for the night in contact with the enemy; the advance was continued before dawn; Segni bridge was found to be blown, but a possible way round close to the Reno floodbank was found to be practicable, though heavily defended, by anti-tank guns and tanks. It was necessary to cross an open quadrilateral of ground, blocked at the far side by a high steep bank; once across this bank, a narrow wedge of land between the Reno and another canal, led on to more open country. At 2 p.m. an attack on the bank was launched by B Squadron; several tanks were knocked out before a Panther, which was doing the damage, was spotted and driven off. Engineers were sent up to blow a gap in the bank; by 4 p.m. the Regiment started to file through the gap. The speed gradually increased, till at 5.30, an undemolished bridge four miles on at Gallo was captured. The news of this was received by Brigade H.Q. with a whoop of joy — 'push on with two squadrons and your infantry to Poggio Renatico — *this is the chance of a lifetime.*' The squadrons took their chance, covering the five miles to Poggio Renatico at full speed on the road. The town was strongly held; the Regiment had to run across the front of a battery of four 88mm anti-aircraft guns, to get into the town. The leading tank was knocked out in the centre of the town, and as dark fell, the Regiment, now exhausted and short of ammunition, leaguered under the walls of the town on a bare field. Enemy vehicles kept approaching from all directions; while orders were being given out at headquarters, a column of transport accompanying a large towed gun appeared from the direction of Segni. Captain Richard Main, the Adjutant, was sent in his tank to deal with it; he drove over and destroyed the column, but on the way back ran into a party of infantry, who burst a grenade on his tank, knocking out most of his teeth; in great pain, and speechless, he carried on all that night and the next day; and was awarded the M.C. Before dawn next morning, after a restless night full of alarms and attacks, 7th Rifle Brigade captured and cleared the town; the battle gradually died down.

On April 20, the Germans had decided to withdraw north of the Po, leaving rearguards on the lines of the water-obstacles. The breakthrough at Segni had out-flanked the rearguard, while the arrival of tanks at Poggio Renatico prevented the withdrawal of all troops south of the Reno. To the north, the 16th/5th Lancers had reached Mirabello, while the Lothians were on the outskirts of Bondeno. After refuelling, the advance was continued westwards, until the two Armies met beyond San Agostino. The leading troop of C Squadron saw tanks coming up the road from the south; a seventeen-pounder shot was fired; fortunately it missed, since the target was American. For the 17th/21st, it was the last shot of the war.

Two days later, all the Germans south of the Po capitulated; on May 2 General Vietinghoff surrendered the German forces in Italy; a week later, the war in Europe ended.

For the Regiment it had been a glorious finish; one D.S.O., four M.C.s and three M.M.s were awarded for this one battle. After a few days' rest, during which two squadrons were changed to armoured cars, the Regiment moved north to begin the task of clearing up in Austria; after the simplicity of war, the complications of peace.

Chapter Fifteen

The Postwar Years

ALTHOUGH THE WAR in Europe was over, two more years were to pass before the Regiment returned to the calm of home service. First came an intense period of clearing up in Austria, where the country was full of armed men, and of abandoned weapons. Refugees, war criminals, young S.S. fanatics, spies, collaborators, deserters, roamed the woods and hills in search of food, shelter, or political asylum. Each Allied unit took charge of a huge area of country, and set about the task of searching out and sorting the human and material debris of war. The 'bag' was both varied and fascinating; secret weapons, forged currency, opulent motor cars, race horses, and many other treasures were found; generally these were grudgingly handed over to higher authority, but sometimes they could be retained, for a time, for regimental use. A small stable of horses was collected, together with some Cossack refugees to look after them. As each area was cleared, the task was begun in another, until gradually the pressure of work began to diminish. This clearing-up process, not unpleasant in the beautiful summer weather, kept all ranks happily occupied, at a time when many units were suffering from reaction; men excited by the prospect of release took readily to looting, and to the selling of stolen army property. In the 17th/21st, three months passed without a single disciplinary case being brought to the Commanding Officer; moreover during the whole war, the War Diary of the

Regiment notes only two courts-martial — surely an outstanding record, which few other units could equal.

The Regiment had lost 21 officers and 135 other ranks killed in the war; 32 officers and over 200 other ranks were wounded; 3 officers and 8 other ranks were taken prisoner. Counting former members of the Regiment serving with the 24th Lancers (formed for the duration of the war) 28 officers and 23 other ranks were decorated for gallantry.

Soon the machinery of demobilization began to move, together with a scheme known as 'Python' by which men still serving were withdrawn to home stations in rotation. As the 17th/21st had been in England until 1942, it was the turn of the Regiment to remain abroad. In October, orders came to move to Greece, to become divisional cavalry regiment to the 4th British Infantry Division. The Regiment spent a cold and thankless winter in Salonika, occupied in famine relief and internal security. Poor accommodation in bad weather, continuous guards and fatigues, the lack of constructive training in the temporary role, coupled with the tremendous drain on the strength of the Regiment by demobilization, Python, leave-in-lieu-of-Python, special end-of-war leave, re-engagement leave, all contributed to bring morale to a very low ebb. The bulk of the Regiment consisted of 500 other ranks from 40th Royal Tank Regiment and 4th Reconnaissance Regiment, mostly awaiting Python; these were later augmented by 250 National Service men.

In October, the Regiment sailed, with relief, away from another Grecian winter, to the warmth of the Suez Canal Zone, where as an armoured car regiment, serious training could be begun again; there was a sharp rise in morale, enhanced by the prospect of more active service. The Regiment was soon ordered to Palestine when, for a year, it was once more to work under conditions of war. Two officers and fourteen other ranks were to give their lives on active service. The difficult and dangerous tasks given to the 17th/21st included the operation of armoured railcars, frontier patrolling, and convoy escort duty. In spite of the constant toll of casualties, morale rose steadily; the Historical Record says, 'the most peaceful individuals, before somewhat half-hearted in their attitude to the

Army, have found in the present more exciting conditions, that the Army is really a good life. Such troops as have been in action, are regarded with envy.' The 17th/21st left Palestine in June 1948, with a farewell message from the G.O.C., General Murray, a former commander of 6th Armoured Division in Italy.

'The comparatively high incidence of deaths and injuries would have undermined seriously the morale of less gifted soldiers. That they continued with their work week after week, in the most trying circumstances, was in accordance with the highest traditions of the service, but is no more than I knew to expect from the officers and men of the 17th/21st Lancers.'

The Regiment arrived home and was stationed at Catterick with the role of Armoured Basic Training Unit, responsible for training newly-arrived recruits in driving and maintenance, gunnery and wireless, a monotonous and repetitive task, of which the only advantage was the opportunity to take the best men out of the National Service intake as instructors. A fine cadre of N.C.O.s was built up, and the Regiment prospered accordingly.

The 17th/21st was now linked permanently to the Nottinghamshire (Sherwood Rangers) Yeomanry, a territorial regiment with a great record in both world wars; it had fought at Gallipoli, and in Greece and Palestine in the first, and at Alamein, in Normandy and on the Rhine in the second. Decorations won in the Second World War included four D.S.O.s, thirty-two M.C.s, a George Medal, three D.C.M.s and thirty-six M.M.s; casualties had included 245 killed and 797 wounded. The affiliation gave the yeomanry regiment a constant source of officers and other ranks for their training cadres, and provided the regular regiment with a fixed recruiting area, in which the regimental representatives were based. This base, now manned by the Regimental Secretary and his staff, is at the Territorial Army Centre, in Sherwood Avenue, Newark, while the Regimental Museum is installed in Belvoir Castle, not far away.

Another regimental affiliation, in force since 1925, is to Lord Strathcona's Horse (Royal Canadian).

After three years at Catterick, the Regiment moved to Chester and later to Salisbury Plain, re-equipped with Comet tanks, in preparation for posting to Germany in December 1951. Since the end of the war, service in Germany has counted as home service for the British Army. Rates of pay and conditions of accommodation rapidly improved after the post-war depression had been overcome. In Germany there were plenty of opportunities for all types of sport for both officers and other ranks. Apart from a certain repetition, unavoidable in peacetime soldiering, life was probably as good in the Army at this period, as it had ever been.

In 1957, Hull, who had been Colonel of the Regiment for ten years, relinquished his appointment. Hull's military career had been an impressive one; after the war he held, among other posts, those of Commandant of the Staff College, Director of Staff Duties, G.O.C. Egypt, Deputy Chief of the Imperial General Staff and was later to become Chief of the Imperial General Staff and Chief of the Defence Staff, in which capacity he was promoted to become the fifth of the Regiment's Field Marshals. In 1959, the bicentenary of the Regiment was celebrated in May with a gathering of Old Comrades, who saw a magnificent parade, on which the C.I.G.S., Sir Gerald Templer, presented a new Guidon to the Regiment. The Guidon, revived after 125 years of disuse, has been reinstated in the cavalry.

In 1960, the Regiment moved to Hong Kong, a cramped and frustrating station for an armoured unit; during this period the Regiment continued its tradition of sending small detachments to odd corners of the world, by deploying five tanks in Borneo, and by sending an officer and fourteen men to serve with the United Nations and 8th U.S. Army Honour Guard at Seoul in Korea.

The Regiment moved to Arabia in 1961, being stationed at Aden, Kuwait, and on a 'Landing Ship Tank' in the Persian Gulf, in the best 'Horse Marine' tradition.

In 1963, the Regiment returned to Germany, to be equipped with what was then the latest of British tanks, the Chieftain. This vehicle was armed with a gun of 120mm, with a greatly improved fire-control system, capable of accuracy both stationary and on the move.

Back in 1945 the Regiment, then in Austria, was ordered to move through the Russian zone to occupy the valley of the River Enns. On the mountain road a vehicle overturned, and the injured, accompanied by the Medical Officer, were taken to a Russian casualty post. The Russian doctor, who was both efficient and friendly, had said, 'What a pity we shall be fighting you next'. This threat of Russian invasion was to hang over Europe for nearly fifty years, and was to dictate the military policy of the NATO Alliance until the sudden dissolution of the Soviet States. The main strength of the British and the Allied Armies was to be concentrated on the defence of the eastern frontier of Germany, by a combination of tactical nuclear weapons, and as powerful a force of tanks as each country concerned could afford.

Germany for a time provided good training areas at Luneburg Heath and Hohne, but as the years went by cross-country movement on the larger exercises became more limited, and the German people increasingly resentful over the damage to their countryside. This problem was relieved to a certain extent by the opening of a fine training area in Alberta in Canada. Here a force of tanks was permanently stationed, and regiments could fly the whole personnel of their battle groups over there for a month every year, and train in manoeuvre and live ammunition firing in 1200 square miles of open country.

Alternating with periods of armoured 'warfare' in Germany, the regiments of the Royal Armoured Corps took turns at some of the remaining commitments of the British Army, in a variety of roles.

Tasks outside the United Kingdom and Germany, from time to time, included a squadron in Cyprus; another in Libya at El Adem the RAF station near Benghazi, a squadron in NATO's Allied Mobile Force, which carried out exercises on the flanks of the main NATO areas as far apart as north Norway, and the Turkish coast; a reconnaissance troupe also served several times in Belize. The Libyan commitment ended with the accession of Colonel Gaddafi, and the removal of all British forces in 1969.

The most demanding of these tasks was the internal security battle against the terrorism of the IRA in Northern Ireland. These 'troubles' — a feature of Irish life for centuries — broke out in July, 1969, and have continued ever since, creating a continual drain on the resources of the Army. It is particularly galling that this task of protection of life and property, impartially on behalf of both Catholic and Protestant factions in the country, is misrepresented abroad, and particularly in America, as a British Colonial occupation and 'oppression' of what is in fact part of the United Kingdom.

In the Northern Irish role, the Regiment was equipped with three squadrons of Saladin armoured cars, Saracen armoured troop carriers, and Ferret scout cars, and an Air Squadron of six helicopters, later increased to twelve.

In 1969 HRH Princess Alexandra was appointed Colonel-in-Chief of the Regiment. There had been no one holding this post since the death of HRH Prince George, Duke of Cambridge, in 1904. He had joined the Regiment as Colonel in 1843, subsequently rising to Field-Marshal and Commander-in-Chief of the British Army.

These duties as an Armoured Reconnaissance Regiment in Ireland occupied the Regiment for two years from 1969 to 1971. To give relief from the dangerous duties in Ireland, individual soldiers were exchanged between Ireland and the Cyprus and Libyan stations.

In 1971 the Regiment returned to Germany, still in the reconnaissance role, as part of the 1st British Corps. However, the Irish troubles continuing, three squadrons in turn returned to Gosford Castle near Armagh, where each spent four months patrolling in Ferret scout cars.

In 1974 the reconnaissance role came to an end and the Regiment was once more converted back to an armoured unit, equipped with Chieftains and allotted to an Armoured Brigade.

At this time the Army Air Corps was given charge of all military helicopters, and armoured reconnaissance regiments no longer operated their own aircraft. This change of policy has remained until the present day, 1993, and constitutes a severe blow to the future of the cavalry. Efforts have been made at various times to

119

allow the cavalry to keep a stake in the helicopter, but without success; it is significant that the American army, for many years lagging behind in tactical development, had decided to equip each armoured division with its own regiment of attack and reconnaissance helicopters. Experience in Vietnam had led to great technical expertise in the development of the 'gunship' as an attack weapon. Any tankman who saw on television the results achieved by these formidable machines against the Iraqi armour in the Gulf War of 1991 must surely have felt a shiver of apprehension as to the future of the tank in open country, if the enemy air forces are still active. The removal of helicopters to a centralized corps in 1974 resulted in an immediate loss of flexibility, at regimental level − a taxi cab on call is not the same as owning one's own car.

In 1975 the Irish problem called once more for extra reinforcements; the whole Regiment spent four months dismounted in the infantry role, in central Belfast, searching buildings, people and vehicles for arms, ammunition and explosives, finally returning again to their tanks in Germany.

In 1977 the Regiment took over for three years as the duty unit at the Royal Armoured Corps centre in Dorset, at Bovington and Lulworth. This task, together with a later one of providing a demonstration squadron at the School of Infantry at Warminster, is a sensible economy, which helps to keep alive the maximum number of armoured regiments in the RAC.

After this period of rather unglamorous duty the Regiment returned to Germany, to be equipped in 1986 with the latest and most expensive modern tank, the Challenger, designed to match the armour of the Warsaw Pact forces. However, in 1989 the whole political atmosphere in Europe was changed by President Gorbachev's *glasnost* and *perestroika*. The separate states of the Soviet Union, and the elements of the Red Army which they contained, began to fragment towards political independence, while increased friendly relations between East and West appeared to remove the threat of war which had so long dominated strategy and tactics in Europe.

In September, 1989, the Regiment, on exercise in Germany,

heard of the death of Field-Marshal Sir Richard Hull and was withdrawn to prepare for the State Funeral. The Field-Marshal being a Knight of the Garter, the ceremony was held at St George's Chapel, Windsor, where his banner was laid up. 107 officers and men, and some twenty members of the Regimental Association took part in the procession while many others attended the moving and impressive service. The Field-Marshal's body was then taken to his home at Pinhoe, Exeter, for burial.

The hopes that the collapse of Russian military strength would bring peace, proved to be ill-founded. Saddam Hussein, dictator of Iraq, relieved of the burden of eight years of unsuccessful war with Iran, decided to make a bid for the domination of the Arabian oil-fields. In August 1990 Iraq invaded Kuwait and appeared likely to go further into Saudi Arabia and the Gulf States.

The United Nations and the United States government produced an amazingly quick reaction by immediately sending troops and aircraft to Saudi Arabia. Great Britain and France agreed to co-operate: 1st Armoured Division was mobilized in great haste, units being below war establishment and depending on the call-up of reservists.

To the intense disappointment of all ranks, the Regiment was not selected to go as a unit, but separate troops of tanks and reconnaissance vehicles were detached to bring up to strength the Queen's Royal Irish Hussars and the Royal Scots Dragoon Guards. They arrived in Arabia by October, and trained in the desert until February 1991, when the land attack on Kuwait began. The Regimental Band also took part in the expedition, in both their musical and medical capacity. The total commitment amounted to five tank troops and over one hundred men.

Operation Granby, the armoured attack on the Iraqi forces in Kuwait was a classic tank manoeuvre − a wide outflanking movement disguised by a huge deception plan, penetrating the outer defences of minefields, ditches, and tanks dug-in in anti-tank role, and then striking at the heart of the enemy's communications.

Although the Regiment did not take part as a whole, or even as a sub-unit − no squadron headquarters was sent out with the detachment — our tank troops were given a leading part in the action, and their gunnery was of the highest standard. Enemy vehicles were destroyed at ranges of over two miles, and in four days the armour covered 350 kilometres to the outskirts of Kuwait City and the Iraq border.

The enemy had been enormously weakened by the complete destruction of their air force, followed by intense and accurate bombing of all visible positions, especially armour dug in as defence, or waiting in reserve. No serious armoured counter-attack was ever developed. But air bombardment, though demoralizing, seldom kills many soldiers, and in the end the ground has to be occupied, enemy troops 'winkled' out of hiding, prisoners taken and removed from the battlefield. Infantry, preceded and supported by tanks are the only agents who can achieve the final result. In this case, the enemy surrendered before street fighting in the city became necessary. Although defeated, Saddam's government still remains intact, and Iran, no longer threatened by Iraq, clearly has ambitions to expand its influence in the area; the Gulf War may well not be the last of the desert campaigns.

Meanwhile, severe recession in all European countries and in the United States of America called for immediate reductions in army budgets, and the consequent vain hope for the production of a 'peace dividend'.

In 1991 the Government instituted the dreaded 'Options for Change' the plan for reduction of the Armed Forces. Disbandments were considered, but rejected in favour of amalgamations in all branches of the Army. Lip service was paid to the Regimental system by the politicians, but no amount of wishful thinking will get away from the fact that if two named regiments are fused into one and given a new name, the Army has lost something irreplaceable forever.

The Cavalry and Royal Tank Regiments were ordered to reduce from nineteen regiments to eleven, and were told to work out how to do this among themselves. The 17th/21st was to amalgamate with the 16th/5th Lancers, and to be renamed The Queen's Royal Lancers. The process was to be completed by June, 1993.

While the Gulf War was still in progress, the Regiment withdrew from Germany, to be stationed at Tidworth until amalgamation had been completed. This process has been tackled with the lessons of the past kept well to the fore. The two Regiments were brigaded together for the whole of World War II, fighting side by side in North Africa and Italy. John Hale's Motto is to remain the Regiment's cap badge, but backed on all other insignia by the crossed lances of Aliwal. Compromises on uniform have been agreed; there will be many more on customs, traditions, and way of life of all ranks, which may take some time to resolve. Her Majesty the Queen will be Colonel-in-Chief of the new Regiment, with HRH Princess Alexandra as her Deputy. In 1922 efforts were made to retain a separate squadron of 21st Lancers. In 1993 the union will be on an equal basis at all levels, one for one in every job. Amalgamation is probably more painful to the Old Comrades than to the serving soldiers, and the union of Regimental Associations can be a difficult process.

When amalgamation is complete the new Regiment moves to Germany, as an armoured regiment equipped with Challenger tanks.

Where the future of the cavalry lies is uncertain: at present the only two roles available are in armour or reconnaissance. The heavy battle tank may well be too expensive (at £3 million each) together with its need for cumbersome transporters. Anti-tank weapons, especially airborne, have become horribly efficient; a single hit may mean complete disintegration of the vehicle, with no hope for the crew.

From the Boer War to the start of World War II, the cavalry had very rarely been the shock arm in attack but had reverted to the roles of reconnaissance and mounted infantry, flank guards, rear guards or advancing rapidly and seizing vital unoccupied ground, but unable to deliver attacks upon defended positions. Mechanization restored their offensive role as they rode into battle, armoured and armed with a gun capable of use in both anti-tank and artillery role. Yet they have always been prepared to leave their tanks and operate on foot, as in the mountains of Italy and in the streets of Northern Ireland. It may well be that this mobile role suitably mounted could be an invaluable additional task for the future rather than risk further contraction as the heavy tank is no longer needed in such large numbers.

The Regimental system is anathema to the bureaucrat and in World War II considerable efforts were made by the Adjutant-General's department to submerge regimental identities into a Corps, and this process continues gradually but inexorably. It can be argued that other nations do without the regimental system, but other nations are not the same as Britain. The Briton likes to belong to a small family group, not to be a cog in a state machine, or a number in a card index. The failure of nationalized industries to do better than private enterprise is symptomatic of this British characteristic. The Defence Ministry must solve the problem of equating the spirit of the small regiment with the administrative simplicity of the larger unit.

The strength of the Cavalry lies in a tradition of speed of movement, speed of thought, mobility and flexibility. They must not attempt to stick to any particular role with the same obstinacy, with which they fought to keep their horses between World Wars I and II.

The world is very far from being at peace: civil war rages in Yugoslavia; the United Nations have large troop concentrations in Cambodia facing an uncompromising Khmer Rouge; a further U.N. military presence has arrived in Somalia; Angola has a rebel uprising; in the remnants of the USSR there are local quarrels; the Red Army, though dispersed, is still the largest in the world, and could very well form the only coherent political element in the country; a military coup might bring back the threat from the east.

One thing is certain; whatever they are asked to do, and wherever they are asked to go, the men who wear the Death's Head Motto will carry out their orders as they have always done, honourably, efficiently and cheerfully.

Appendix I

Stations

17TH LIGHT DRAGOONS

1759	Watford and Rickmansworth – Coventry.
1760-4	Scotland, Ireland
1775-9	Boston, America, Halifax, Nova Scotia. New York, Philadelphia. Long Island – detachment to Carolina.
1784	Ireland.
1795-6	Jamaica, San Domingo, Grenada.
1797-1801	Trowbridge, Nottingham, Gloucester, Bath, Bristol, Canterbury, Manchester.
1803	Ireland.
1806	Brighton, Romsey, Rye, Hastings.
1807	River Plate, S. America.
1808	Portsmouth, Chichester, and to India.
1809	India.

17TH LANCERS

1823	Chatham and home service.
1828	Ireland.
1832-7	Gloucestershire, Hounslow, Leeds and Burnley, Manchester, Norwich and Ipswich, Coventry, Northampton.
1838	Ireland.

1841-5	Glasgow and Edinburgh, Leeds, Nottingham, Hounslow and Brighton.
1847	Ireland.
1851	Woolwich, Canterbury and home service.
1854	Kulali, Varna, and the Crimea.
1856	Ireland.
1858	Bombay.
1859	Gwalior.
1860	Secunderabad.
1865-9	Colchester, Aldershot, Brighton, Shorncliffe, Woolwich, Kensington, Hampton Court, Edinburgh.
1870	Ireland.
1876-8	Aldershot and Leeds.
1879	S. Africa and India.
1880-4	Mhow, Lucknow.
1890-4	Shorncliffe (one sqn in Egypt) and home.
1897	Ireland.
1900	Aldershot − South Africa.
1902	Edinburgh and Glasgow
1905	India − Meerut and Sialkot.
1914-1918	France and Flanders.
1919	Cologne.
1920	Ireland.
1922	Tidworth. Amalgamation with 21st Lancers.

21ST (GRANBY'S) LIGHT DRAGOONS

1760	Nottinghamshire.
1763	Disbanded.

21ST (BEAUMONT'S) LIGHT DRAGOONS

1794	Yorkshire.
1796	San Domingo.
1798	Home service.
1806	Cape of Good Hope, S. Africa. Detachment to River Plate, S. America.

126

1808	Detachment to Madeira.
1815	Detachments to St. Helena and Tristan da Cunha.
1817	India.
1819	England – disbanded.

21ST HUSSARS

1857	India.
1873	England.
1881	Ireland.
1884	Detachment to Khartoum.
1888	India.
1896	Egypt and Sudan.

21ST LANCERS

1899	Home service.
1912	India.
1916	North-west Frontier. Detachment to France and Flanders.
1921	Home service – disbanded.
1922	One squadron reformed and amalgamated with 17th Lancers.

17TH/21ST LANCERS

1922	Tidworth.
1925	Aldershot.
1928	Hounslow.
1930	Egypt – Cairo.
1932	India – Secunderabad.
1935	Meerut.
1939	Colchester, and home service.
1942	Algeria and Tunisia.
1944	Italy.
1945	Austria.
1946	Greece.
1947	Suez Canal Zone, Palestine, Catterick.
1951	Germany.
1960	Hong Kong.

1961	Aden, Kuwait, Persian Gulf.
1963	Germany.
1969	N. Ireland; squadrons in Libya and Cyprus.
1971	Germany; duty squadron in N. Ireland.
1975	N. Ireland.
1976	Germany.
1977	R.A.C. Centre, Bovington; detachment with NATO.
1980	Germany.
1990	Tidworth; detachments to Gulf War.
1993	Amalgamation with 16th/5th Royal Lancers.

Appendix II

Battle Honours

THE 17TH (DUKE OF CAMBRIDGE'S OWN) LANCERS

Alma	Inkerman
Balaclava	Sebastopol

Central India
South Africa 1879
South Africa 1900-1902

France and Flanders 1914-1918

Festubert 1914	Lys
Somme 1916-1918	Hazebrouck
Morval	Amiens
Cambrai 1917, 1918	*Hindenburg Line*
St. Quentin	*St. Quentin Canal*
Avre	*Beaurevoir*

Pursuit to Mons

THE 21ST (EMPRESS OF INDIA'S) LANCERS
Khartoum
North-West Frontier, India, 1915, 1916

THE 17TH/21ST LANCERS

North Africa 1942-1943	Italy 1944-1945
Tebourba Gap	Cassino II
Bou Arada	*Monte Piccolo*

Kasserine	Capture of Perugia
Thala	*Advance to Florence*
Fondouk	Argenta Gap
El Kourzia	*Fossa Cembalina*
Tunis	
Hammam Lif	

Honours in roman type are not borne on the Guidon, since regiments are restricted to ten honours for each of the two world wars, for emblazonment on Colours, etc.

Appendix III

Notes On Dress
Of The Regiment

The table overleaf has kindly been compiled for me by Major
G.A.S. Graham, MBE, the Regimental Secretary.

It aims to give only the broad outline of the main changes of
dress in the Regiment — to follow all the details would require a
book as long as this short history. Full details can be found in Vols.
I and II of the Regimental History.

To help any reader who is unfamiliar with the details of military
dress, this illustration, taken from the picture on page 77 gives the
main items of clothing and saddlery of a mounted officer.

131

Dress of the 17th Lancers

Tunic – 1759 Scarlet, 1784 blue, 1810 French grey, 1814 Blue (cavalry grey in India), 1830 red, 1840 blue, 1872 blue with reversible 'plastron' front, 1879 (India) Khaki drill (white review order), 1888 blue drill serge with white piping, 1890 blue, white collar, yellow cord shoulder straps, 1900 (South Africa) Khaki frock with brass numerals, 1902 khaki serge, stand collar, 1902 ORs' blue serge with white gorget patch on collar, shoulder chains, 1914 service dress khaki with brass collar badges.

Facings – 1759 white, 1814 white lapels buttoned back, 1829 no facings, 1830 white, 1855-56 top corners of lapels turned back to show white, 1872 plastron, white in review order, blue marching order.

Trousers – 1759 grey white pantaloon, high soft boots, 1810 blue-grey pantaloon, Hessian boots, 1814 white pantaloon, 1829 'Oxford mixture' (grey-black), 1830 blue, double red stripe, 1840 Oxford mixture, (Crimea) grey, double white stripe (often leathered up to knee), 1855 blue, double white stripe, 1872 knee boots, 1900 (South Africa) khaki breeches, puttees, unblacked boots, 1902 khaki serge with puttees, 1914 cord riding breeches, brown riding boots for officers, puttees for ORs.

Headdress – 1759 Brown light dragoon helmet with fur at bottom.

Crossbones above skull, 1789 leather, fur crossing from front to rear, hackle plume on left, small badge on right. 1806 tall brown felt shako, white lace, badge in front, red and white plume above it, 1823 lance cap, red and white plume, 1830 black cock's feather plume (officers), black horsehair ORs, 1854 black oilskin case for marching order, 1855 white plume, 1857 (India) leather forage cap without peak, cloth cover protecting neck. 1869 black plume, 1871 white plume, 1879 (India) khaki or white helmet with brass spike, 1900 (South Africa) white helmet with khaki cover, 1902 blue and white peaked forage cap (khaki for marching order) blue and white 'side hat'. 1914 steel helmet.

Shabracque – 1759 red, 1769 white (no badge), 1810 blue with tassels, 1823 lances added to Royal Cypher, white sheepskin with blue edge, 1827 black sheepskin for officers, 1830 plainer shabracque, 1833 black sheepskin for all ranks. 1867 black shabracque, 1869 white, 1872 shabracque abolished for ORs, 1890 gold-laced, black sheepskin with white edge, 1896 abolished.

Other Saddlery –1810 black leather sabretache, 1814 valises introduced. 1827 sabretache abolished for ORs, 1896 sabretache and valises abolished.

Pouch belts – 1814 silver lace, 1830 gold lace with white stripe.

Gauntlets – introduced 1833.

Dress of 21st Lancers

1760-1763 (Granby's Regiment) – scarlet, dark blue facings; light dragoon helmet with RF badge (Royal Foresters).

1779-1783 (Douglas' Regiment) scarlet, white facings; black leather helmet, bearskin crest.

1794-1819 (Beaumont's Regiment) blue, facings yellow 1794, pink 1814, black 1815, light dragoon helmet till 1812, then felt shako.

1861 (21st Hussars) blue, grey facings – busby with grey bag.

1897 (21st Lancers) blue, grey facings red in 1897 till after

Omdurman). Lance cap, white plume, badge VRI with crossed lances.

Dress of 17th/21st Lancers

1922 Amalgamation, 21st Lancer Sqn. wore own uniform till 1929.

1930-38 (India) khaki drill (summer) service dress (winter).

1939 Serge battle dress, khaki side hat.

1942-45 Denim or serge battledress, tank suits, black berets.

1954 No. 1 Dress (blues) issued to sergeants and NCOs.

1956 New officers mess kit authorized — blue, white, facings and piping.

1960 (Far East) white tropical jackets for ceremonial parades, khaki drill for normal work.

1961 No. 2 Dress (service dress) issued to whole Army.

1963 Battle dress replaced by green sateen combat dress.

Appendix IV

Armour Used By The Regiment Since 1939

UK: Mk.III"Valentine"IV 40mm 17t

UK: Mk.VI"Crusader"I 40mm 19t

US: M4A4"Sherman" 75mm 36t

"Sherman" 17pr Armour: Max 76mm Min 25mm

UK: "Comet"I 77mm 33t

UK: "Cromwell" VII 75mm 28t

UK: SALADIN

UK: SARACEN

UK: "Centurion"Mk.5 83.4mm 50t

UK: "Conqueror"Mk.3 120mm 65t

UK: "Chieftain" 120mm 50t

U K : "Challenger" 120mm

INDEX